Linda

Owslebury Bottom

OWSLEBURY BOTTOM

Peter Hewett

DRAWINGS BY ROSIE NEWMAN

THE SUMACH PRESS

First published in Great Britain in 1991 by
The Sumach Press
29 Mount Pleasant, St. Albans, Herts AL3 4QY

British Library Cataloguing in Publication Data

Hewett, Peter
Owslebury Bottom.
I. Title
920

ISBN 0-7126-5012-1

Photoset in Linotronic Baskerville by
SX Composing Ltd, Rayleigh, Essex.
Printed and bound in Great Britain by
Mackays of Chatham.

CONTENTS

PART FIVE *Paradise Gained and Lost*

FOREWORD

My memory is becoming treacherous. I am not so good at names any more, I can't remember my dreams when I wake, I get mixed up. But some things are indelible, some things change your life . . .

I had been a pupil of the local grammar school for only a few awestruck days when an incident occurred which must have been instantly forgotten by all the protagonists except me, and yet in my eleven-year-old world, nothing would ever be the same.

A chattering classroom of black-blazered boys was silenced a few moments after returning from morning assembly by the arrival of a small, furious black-haired teacher wearing a thick brown suit which was much too hot for that sunny morning. 'Where is he, where is he?' we heard him fulminating in exaggerated distress, as we all paled in panicky respect for this hitherto unknown member of staff. Suddenly his eyes dilated, and refocused on me at my desk towards the back of the classroom.

'You,' he bellowed, pointing inescapably at me like Kitchener. 'You, boy – talking through assembly! We'll have to teach you a lesson. You can't behave like that in a school like this. You're in detention tonight!' His gown billowed behind him as he went like an angry wasp out of the stunned room.

I stood still for a few moments as my horrified brain, re-activated from a thrumming paralysis, understood that this was a case of mistaken identity. I had uttered not a word through those prayers and announcements, but something that sounded like a jail sentence had been irreversibly and unfairly imposed upon me, disgracing my parents, and blighting my future. Then I started sobbing, convulsing like a baby, almost unable to breathe.

When I next became aware of anything other than the end of the world, I realised I was being spoken to by a quiet, confessional voice. 'Oh dear, oh dear. What's the matter here? Come on, old chap, tell me what this is about.' The gentle voice hushed a flurry of falsetto witnesses, and with infinite patience began to piece together my story like fragments of a Dead Sea Scroll from my grief-wracked evidence.

At last, I calmed sufficiently to open my eyes. My confessor was sitting on the desk next to mine and leaning over me. His eyes were sad and yet faintly twinkling from behind the thick lenses of his spectacles. His greying hair was brushed back with no parting from his expansive forehead. He smiled.

'Cheer up, old chap. I'll see what can be done.'

He ordered the class to open their 'reader' for the term and to study the first chapter in silence while he was away. Only the sniffs and snuffles of my exhausted distress broke the quiet of the next few minutes. When he returned, he came straight up to my desk and said loud enough for all to hear, 'It's all sorted out. You don't have to be in detention. It was a mistake.'

My tears ran into my smiling mouth which was opening and closing in short and shallow gulps. Relief and a sense of vindication coalesced into a vow that I would do anything to repay this man who had become the idol of my juvenile life.

He had stepped back to the front of the class. He turned to Form 1A2 and said, 'Well, now, let's start again. I am going to teach you English and my name is Mr Hewett.'

I suspect that had my saviour told us that he was to teach us Needlework, I would have spent my life as a dressmaker, so entirely was I dominated by the necessity of emulating and pleasing him. But not only did he teach us English, he was also the presiding and organising energy which produced the school plays, so that my duty and desire were united whenever I was able to take part.

As a teacher, he was magnetic; never raising his voice, he expanded our love of language and our vocabulary through the example of his wit, his fervour and his pleasure. By the time I was one of his hushed pupils, the derivation of his school nickname was lost, but I always felt it was satisfying and funny that so sophisticated and so civilised a man should be referred to by hundreds of schoolboys as 'Stan'.

He loved questions, his language became more vernacular, his imagery spontaneous when he sensed interest, or challenge. He told stories full of characters with accents and dialects, he especially enjoyed laughing at East Anglian vowels, but then the return of seriousness would be signalled by a ritual nudging with a forefinger of his spectacles back up to their exact resting place on the bridge of his nose, immediately followed by a contemplation of the fingernails of that hand, which were always and without exception pared and clean. His control was absolute, of his subject, of his mood and of us.

As a producer of plays, the carapace of the teacher became transparent and some of the off-duty man emerged, smoking Players Weights, addressing his junior thespians as 'mate' and 'chum' and finding laughter in every part of the stamina-draining process.

The school was unusually interested in drama, an interest which extended beyond Shakespeare and other 'suitable' classics to an annual variety show performed by the masters, requiring occasional help from the boys. I managed to get myself involved in these impromptus as well and began to attend rehearsals where Mr Hewett was instructing his colleagues. On these occasions, teachers with institutionalised nicknames like Meph, Pot, Spike and Fishy, became David, John, Michael and Jack to each other within our amazed hearing, and Stan became Peter.

My contribution to these reviews was very small, but I watched every moment of the teachers' rehearsals and yearned to be included one day in their discussions and banter, their games of association, their yarns and their skill. I observed Peter Hewett accepting other people's suggestions; combining ideas; easing the tension; taking the responsibility; and slowly it dawned on me, at the age of fifteen, that he was being a director, and that being a director was what I wanted to do with my life.

In the sixth form, Mr Hewett became our conscience, leading daily debates on the political, social and moral changes happening around us. He lent us his copies of the *New Statesman*, he talked about girls and contraception, he got us listening to Bach and Mozart while delighting in news of the rock-and-roll group five of us had formed, he recounted tales of legendary stage performances in Stratford and at the Old Vic, he made us understand the bravery of pacifism, and he gave us our pride in state education and the courage of our convictions.

He wrote on our blackboard a line from Dante to show us that contradiction was a key to understanding our lives:

En la sua voluntade, e nostra pace.

In his absence, one of us wrote an irreverent translation underneath:

Our park-keeper enjoys free love.

When he saw it, he roared with laughter and asked us to leave it there because it was a statement of equally profound gravitas.

By then, a few of us were taking Literature as a scholarship-level subject. Peter suggested we attach ourselves to an extra-mural course he was teaching on Friday nights at his village hall – the sort of work that was to lead to his pioneering involvement with the Open University.

Those Friday nights were exhilarating. We were studying, but we were no longer in school uniforms. Not only were the sessions on Shakespeare extraordinarily illuminating because the discussions Peter provoked were inclusively adult, but the atmosphere had a conviviality which at the end of each seminar led us *en masse* down the dark lanes and into the pub. Peter called us by our first names, we smoked cigarettes, drank beer and talked and talked and talked . . .

He lived nearby, surrounded by cornfields in a converted windmill where, until the early hours, we gathered around his glowing hearth, an elated extended family playing our music, testing him with our jokes and realising that not only was our teacher human, but we were too.

Peter and his wife, Diana, would often invite me to stay over. That passion for all the works of nature which so informed his teaching became more real to me as I watched him notating every changing detail of his Suffolk habitat. I thought then what I have found to be true ever since: everything in Peter's life connects, everything contributes to a sense of richness, intensity and fertility so that literature and drama are part of how he lives, not separate from it. That was the time he showed me the poems of Gerard Manley Hopkins, and the novels of D.H. Lawrence; that was the time we read *The Winter's Tale* . . .

By then it was clear that he had become determined about my future. He devoted endless extra-curricular hours to my preparation for an Open Scholarship Examination at Cambridge; he offered my parents financial assistance, even threatening resignation when a charitable grant was to be denied me; he set me mock papers, ruthlessly attacked my weaknesses, shamelessly taught me tricks of examination survival and fervently eradicated my self-doubt with a mixture of good advice and bad language.

And so the sweetest and most indelible memory of my youth is a sound, no picture. I was in a freezing cold telephone box because we had no phone at home; I had just pressed button A and told Peter that I had received a telegram from Downing College, Cambridge awarding me a scholarship. There was a shout, then a beat of silence and then I heard him whisper, 'We did it . . .'. *We* did, indeed.

Reading *Owslebury Bottom* has made me realise all over again how blessed I was, we all were, to have our lives shaped by such a life-loving, life-inducing man. This minutely detailed evocation of a magical time in his childhood reveals a novelist's delight in characters, a poet's intense fascination with the miraculous minutiae of nature, and above all the man himself, utterly honest, completely good, unfailingly aware, openly emotional and truly human. Peter loves the moments in literature when what is apparently simple resonates with many levels of meaning. It is, I have always thought, truly appropriate that one of his favourite lines is Hamlet's, summarising his father's life:

He was a man. Take him for all in all.

TREVOR NUNN
1991

PREFACE

The Hampshire village where I spent my early childhood is Owslebury, pronounced Ozzle-berry, not Owls-berry.

This book is based on my personal recollections of life in what was then an isolated village. There was no radio, television, public transport or, as far as I remember, even a newspaper or telephone to link us to the outer world. The book is a picture of how I remember it, and if it has achieved its own authenticity I shall be happy indeed.

I've changed most of the names of people but retained place names where possible. I have since discovered that I misunderstood at least one important fact of village life, but it is truth to my memories and my feelings that is my concern. The preoccupation with collecting birds' eggs and butterflies belongs very much to that period, when both were warmly approved by teachers and parents, and widespread if not universal among country children. Here in East Anglia I have helped to found the local branch of the Suffolk Wildlife Trust and I chaired the branch for eleven years. This, I think, sufficiently shows how much I now disapprove of such collecting.

I owe warmest thanks to the following: Trevor Nunn for writing the Foreword to this book which I value greatly, embarrassingly flattering though it is; Alan Hill for being an invaluable help as an unpaid agent and for finding me a publisher; Mick Wilson for continual encouragement and support; Betty Harfield of Owslebury for helping with both photographs and place names; Heather Godwin of The

Sumach Press for liking the book and being a strong moral and literary support; and lastly my wife Diana for reordering the chaotic material, typing several drafts from end to end, and being throughout an indispensible helpmeet and colleague. Without her, *Owslebury Bottom* would never have been finished.

PART ONE

Early Days

CHAPTER ONE

SNAPSHOT

It is early in February 1922. The little room is warm to the point of stuffiness; outside the cottage it is cold and promising frost, though the plum tree in the front garden, striped with light from the gaps in the curtains, is already in blossom. The basket fire, flanked by its oven, is glowing with coal and crackling with wood. It takes up one side of the room with its attendant cupboards and shelves. Small twigs and a scattering of dead matchsticks on the brick hearth throw minute shadows when the fire flares. To the right of the fireplace is a built-in sofa covered with blankets and cushions. Three children sit there in a row, their faces occasionally vivid as a hissing flame lights them. The girl is ten years old – and high-coloured, excitable, fidgety; her hair is in plaits with bright red bows, and is tightly drawn from her face; she has prominent front teeth and is knitting vigorously but with some difficulty. At the other end of the settee is a small snub-nosed boy of five, sleepy and indeed soon to be taken to bed, but at present propping up his eyelids and playing quietly with a toy train made of pale wood. He is wheeling this up and down the settee and it makes a tiny wooden noise. In the middle is me. I am nearly eight years old. I am not doing anything except listening. On one corner of the large oblong table is an oil lamp; it makes attractive dim images in the corners of the room, but casts a sharp circle of bright light on to the ceiling and another on to the table. On this table is a large drawing board with irregular-shaped bits of cardboard and a litter of pots, jars, tins, brushes, and pencils. My father sits within this circle of light cutting card with a slender-bladed knife: he too is listening. Just inside the circle, straining her eyes over the small print, my mother, Florence, is reading aloud from *Great Expectations*, about Wemmick's castle. We keep several bashed-up volumes of Dickens in the cupboard over the front door, where most of our books are stored. This one is published by Chapman and Hall and dated 1868: the cover has a red bumpy surface and on its front, a gold embossed reproduction of Charles Dickens's signature with multiple underlinings as a flourish. The illustrations are not by the artists my father prefers, but I still like them, especially the fine cross-hatching. The minute, precise print on thick creamy paper is framed in a thin black rule and headed by running titles in sloping print, also framed, a different one for each page. The spine of the book is broken, some of the leaves are dog-eared and the pictures loose, but only one page is missing. I have a deep affection for this book, and often study the drawings and advertisements at the end, but the text is too long and difficult for me to read on my own, so I listen. I am mystified, fascinated, silent . . . Part of my mind is on birds and birds' nests, but most of it is at Walworth with the Aged P. There is no other sound but the shifting and settling of the fire and Florence's quiet voice. There is a strong smell of home-made cigarettes, one of which has just gone out in my father's tin.

'One more chapter?' asks my mother. All of us on the sofa shout, 'Yes!' and even though Bill is struggling to keep his eyes open, he shouts the loudest. The fire sighs and settles, and a momentary puff of gas burns blue. The window is misted up with steam, and in spite of the warm overhang of thatch there is now a wafer-thin layer of frost on the panes outside. A column of smoke climbs straight upwards from the brick chimney in the cold air. A star or two twinkles in the dark sky and the yellow crescent moon is just above the horizon. A tawny owl calls quaveringly from Gough's Lane; there is a small flurry in the hedge beyond the Shearer's Arms where a weasel is suckling its new-born litter. Inside the warm room my father lights another wispy fag and bends again to his work; Joan clicks her needles, Bill shuffles his train wheels and yawns, and there is a rustle as Florence turns the page and reads on.

CHAPTER TWO

FINDING OUR FEET

My parents came from strikingly different backgrounds. My father, Arthur James Hewett, was the youngest of a family of eight. *His* father, George, was a skilled joiner living in Dulwich, and all the brothers became craftsmen except for the youngest, Arthur, the runt, who showed early talent as an artist. In due course he obtained a place to study at the Camberwell School of Art. It was perhaps inevitable that he quickly began to see himself as superior to the rest of the family, if not to the world in general. It was he who took pride in a family legend that Charles Dickens was his great uncle, and he believed he had inherited some talent from that source; throughout his life he told long and complex stories of a vaguely Dickensian cast.

My mother, in contrast, was middle class: *her* father, Arthur Seymour Jennings, was a prosperous journalist who edited a successful trade-paper in the City and lived in a large house at the much posher end of Dulwich. Florence Margeurite was the first-born, and her birthplace was Yonkers, New York. Her mother, Jenny, was American, and had been wooed and married by ASJ during a long business visit to America.

Florence went to Haberdashers Askes School. When she was seventeen she was cycling down Barry Road one day on her way home when her chain slipped. She propped the bicycle against the kerb and was trying to put the chain back and getting a bit oily in the process, when a striking figure stopped and offered to help her. It was Arthur. He was twenty-three, a romantic figure with red hair who wore a tall hat and a frock coat. He was a commercial artist in the city. They met surreptitiously for some weeks until Florence plucked up enough courage to take him home and introduce him to the formidable ASJ, who clearly didn't think much of Florence's beau. In his view he was too old for her, had rather poor prospects, and was socially inferior – even though he talked very posh indeed.

The early confrontations between ASJ and Arthur contained some rather strained passages of dialogue; Florence swore, for example, that one of Arthur's attempts at polite conversation was 'Perhaps you know St John's Church, which is somewhat picturesquely situated on Goose Green?'

ASJ was a devious character, and instead of shouting or complaining when it was clear that Florence would not give Arthur up, he sent her away for a whole year to the Scilly Isles, where a friend owned a hotel. St Mary's was not only highly suitable as an 'Island of Shalott' for Florence, giving her time to reflect, but was also an ideal place to distract her, as it was a port of call for certain Atlantic ships, and the scene that year of more than one naval wreck. Her hotel was therefore full for weeks at a time of dashing young officers and captains. However, she resisted all their flatteries and blandishments, and sustained firmly her love for her small verbose suitor. When the year was over, ASJ admitted defeat and reluctantly allowed the wedding to go ahead.

My parents started their married life in a little house in Undercliffe Road, Lewisham; my father buckled down to his job as a commercial artist, and by the time the Great War started there were two children in the family. Arthur, in common with most men of his generation, had very little to do with his children when they were babies – he left all that to Florence. So I have no memory of missing him when he joined the army under the Derby Scheme in 1916. In the spring of 1917 he was being trained for overseas service in a camp at Hazeley Down near Winchester. He had hoped to be able to join the Artists' Rifles but instead found himself in an infantry regiment, the Twentieth London.

Rumours of increased Zeppelin raids on South East London reached him and he became worried about the safety of his young family. He decided to evacuate us, and found temporary lodgings for us all (Bill had been born in the January of that year) in the nearby village of Twyford. Here we lodged with a large family, and the boy I slept with smelt strongly of cabbage. We played by a pond where a retired major shouted to his grandchildren 'Come in, you little BUGGahs!', and we heard the story of the schools medical inspector who couldn't examine a Twyford schoolboy because he was 'sewn up for the winter'; not only his one-piece woollen undergarment but his waistcoat were sewed up with the intention that he would be warm until April. Once, Joan and I sat on the curved and lichened coping-stones of a wall listening with three-quarters horror and one-quarter fascination to the sound of pigs being killed a few barns away; mercifully we could see nothing. Eating pig's lard on bread a couple of days later was delicious in spite of knowing where it had so recently come from. It was while we were here that my father left for the trenches in France. Florence decided to stay in the country, and, hearing of a two-bedroom empty cottage in Owslebury, a small village lying to the south, she left us children with her landlady, walked to see the cottage, instantly took it at half a crown a week, sent for the furniture, and moved in. Our furniture, what there was of it, was balanced uneasily and roped on to a cart which swayed perilously on the way down the hill to Owslebury Bottom.

The cottage was on a gentle slope, part of a settlement too small to be called a hamlet – a pub, a few scattered houses casually strung along the road and up lanes, and two farms. Owslebury itself (population 200, church, school, two shops) was nearly a mile away, cut off from us by a steepish hill. In spite of boasting two bedrooms (however tiny and low), the cottage looked very small, and attached to it was another identical cottage occupied by an oldish couple called the Nevilles. We had what seemed to me a large garden, casual and tapering in shape. Almost all of it ran to the side of the house and was marked off by a hedge of elder, dogwood, privet and my favourite wayfaring tree, with flat umbels of flower and good red berries; this hedge was masked with ivy and bramble and faded out into a little patch of birch saplings and old hawthorns. At the front there was a small stiff wicket gate, originally painted white, flanked on the left by bushes of flowering currant and lilac. On the right was the well, with rope and windlass, our only source of water, cold and delicious. It was especially exciting when the sun or the moon made a half circle down in the bricky depths as I leaned over the high circular edge. A path led to a rickety wooden porch and the front door which opened straight and draughtily into the sitting room. The roof was straw thatch, ancient and mossy at the back, relatively fresh at the front, though it wasn't wired and therefore had become a nursery for sparrows and starlings which chattered and cheeped all the year round and at dawn, seemed to stamp about in spacious interior chambers somewhere inside the thatch. Not far from the house was a large tumbledown barn with tarred wooden walls and a couple of webby windows. Its roof still had sturdy-looking eaves, but some of the pantiles had slipped or been blown down, leaving tile-shaped gaps here and there. The lavatory, which was near the barn, was wood and tile. It was an earth closet two-seater (I couldn't think why anyone would ever want to share) and, though whitewashed, was liable to be occupied by immense and grisly spiders. I had a persistent nightmare about opening the door and finding an Old Man sitting there. The back of the cottage faced a nearby vertical bank of earth, and part of the little space between was spanned with corrugated iron, pocked with rust and patched with lichen on its promontories and with wild oats sprouting here and there in its valleys. But there was room for two enormous cankered apple trees, which leant over the house and were weighed down in autumn with sweet but spotty fruit. The apples often lodged in the concavities, but the whole contraption was dangerous to step on, so we dislodged promising-looking ones with sticks, and caught them as they tumbled down the valleys. This steep bank ran down the length of the garden, and earth steps, shored up with old timber, led steeply up to a meadow of about an acre which went with the house. Behind this lay open fields.

In January we felt totally isolated, but Florence had the kind of pluck and strong nest-making instincts which made us feel cosy and self-supporting rather than lonely. Our little empire was the house, the garden and the Medder – it was always called the Medder and never the Meadow. Even in the hardest weather the butcher and the baker called, and Stan Hutchins, the postman; Frankie Southgate from down the road was a frequent caller who brought us kindling wood and sometimes a rabbit.

Florence held her strongly contrasting children in a cradle of invisible security, watching us but not watching us. I remember her in those early days as tall, slim, prematurely grey-haired, and, I thought, beautiful, smothered in pale face-powder when she was going out; it always seemed to get on her lapels and gloves. She had a splendid energy, was scarcely ever daunted – and would try anything at least once.

Joan's birthday was in August, and when I started school in September at the age of four and a half she seemed to me to be almost one of the grown-ups. As a seven-year-old she had already joined the 'biguns' when I started as a 'littleun'. She was tall, very tall from my eye level and, we said, skinny. She wore her fair hair in two plaits finished with ribbon bows, a different colour for each day of the week.

Most of my early memories of Joan are connected with school, as she took charge of me from the first day. As soon as we left the front gate of the cottage she looked after me, and solved all my problems, as well as carrying my lunch in her satchel. As the weather got colder she had her own ways of keeping us warm, and I was often made to pause half-way up Crabbe's Hill for a little pantomime of running on the spot while making scarecrow movements with my arms. Whenever I had a smut on my nose, a bloodied knee, or ears which she thought wouldn't suffer a close inspection, a corner of my handkerchief, or hers if I hadn't got one, was screwed into a tail-shaped twist; then she put it to my mouth and said, 'Spit.' The ear, nose or knee was then sniggled with the dampened handkerchief and scrubbed dry again. It had to be a twisted corner, and my own spittle, though I didn't understand why.

Joan's loving attentiveness had its snags and even its embarrassments when we were actually at school, but on balance it was valuable and valued. She always got me there on time, though occasionally I had to be dragged as we ran together to reach the school gate before the bell stopped.

Joan was always the responsible one, perhaps because she was a girl as well as the oldest, and thus expected to be. I remember her being desperately keen to lay the table before my mother returned from the long walk up to the village for paraffin and candles, the shopping carried in a basket slung between the handles of the pram, so that she and I would be sitting 'reading' beside the carefully laid table when my mother came up the path, the pram weighed down with dead sticks from the beechwoods.

At school one of my earliest lessons was called 'fraying': we sat listening to the teacher reading bible stories aloud, and pulled little squares cut from woven material into fingers-full of one-way threads. We were not told why, and assumed it was just to keep us quiet; but it was probably for field dressings for the wounded, as the war had not yet ended. As soon as we could manage we were taught – boys as well as girls – to knit, and my first pink duster had such tight stitches that it was as stiff as a board, and was kept in the cottage for a while as a charming joke. Miss Gorman was my first teacher: she wished to seem strict but was soft and sweet not far beneath. When I was very small I was taken on to her lap and cuddled, and I had confused dreams about her really being a man, though the soft and downy face immediately above me was manifestly a woman's. Perhaps I dreamt this because Florence, though she sometimes hugged me, never took me on her lap nowadays, whereas some of my uncles did.

The school and the school house were next to the church, and the churchyard was used unofficially for lunch-time games, being much pleasanter, with its grass and old yew trees, than the barren desert of the playground. The yews were vast and either sprawling or surprisingly and bulkily upright, the former offering good hiding-places. We would crouch among the strong-smelling needles and against the gnarled pinkish-brown of the main trunk. The tiny yellow bobbles of the flowers were not like any others I had seen, and the soft distinctively-shaped red fruits had an appeal of their own, though we felt they might poison us merely by being looked at; we were all firmly trained in the dangers of poisonous plants and feared the mere presence of deadly nightshade berries. The churchyard also had interesting hazards in the way of headstones and grave-surrounds and even railings around tombs which we used as climbing frames. One thing we all half-believed was that if you walked round the kerb of a certain gravestone exactly seven times and then immediately put your ear to the stone, you would hear the devil. I tried fairly often, but I never seemed to be quite quick enough. Once, poor Joan fell from the churchyard wall into a patch of flourishing nettles and got badly stung. Within a minute or two she not only had pink patches but also raised blisters all over her face, arms and legs. Though tears were running down her face she ridiculed the concern we showed; we dashed round finding dock leaves, but she wouldn't let us rub them on her face, though we were allowed to do so on her bare arms and legs, leaving green stains and perhaps making her skin even more painful by our over-zealousness.

I don't remember very much classroom work, but have an impression that there was a good deal of religion, which I vaguely associated with the geographical juxtaposition of church and school. We sang hymns, of course, first thing in the morning after the register was called; the whole school sang these accompanied by Miss Gorman at the dyspeptic harmonium. One very familiar hymn that bothered me a good deal, though for some reason adults didn't ever explain it, started:

> There is a green hill far away
> Without a city wall.

I knew lots of green Hampshire hills and none of them had a city wall, so I thought the second line hardly worth saying. Later in the same hymn we sang:

> There was no other good enough
> To pay the price of sin:

He only could unlock the gates
Of heaven and let us in.

Leaving aside the problem of how much sin cost, which I found tenebrous, the third and fourth lines seemed to me to imply that unlocking the gates of heaven was all *He* could manage, which I thought was quite an achievement. Another had a pleasingly bouncy tune, but one mysterious word. I never asked about this, as I knew perfectly well what it meant, though I couldn't see what it was doing in that context:

Let every creature rise and sing
Peculiar honours to our King.

Even the Lord's Prayer which we said so frequently was full of traps: 'Thy will be done on earth as it is heaven'; I took 'will' as an auxiliary part of the verb 'will be done' and the subject of the sentence as 'thy'; my tongue tripped on it every time I said it. 'Forgive us our trespasses' I thought meant: don't make too much fuss about our going into Schwartz's forest or Marwell Wood where to my eye, it clearly said 'Trespasses will be Prosecuted'. There were corresponding and permanently unsolved problems about the little verse we sang on our knees at bedtime:

Lord keep us safe this night
Secure from all our fear;
May angels guard us while we sleep
Till morning light appear. Amen.

I always sang 'safe' as 'save' and the rhythm of the tune made 'secure' into 'sea-cure', which I associated with the hymn about 'those in peril on the sea', and I was worried about 'appear' which I thought ought to be 'appears', not knowing about the subjunctive, but then it wouldn't rhyme with 'fear'. Both at home and at school, the world of words was full of tripwires, and it was never explained to me why my statement, 'Saul was a gentleman' was greeted with gales of laughter and repeated delightedly to visitors as a kind of *bon mot*.

Mr and Mrs Neville next door had once had a large family but the children had long since left the nest. They were both very supportive in the early days of our arrival; Mrs Neville did some shopping for us at intervals and Mr Neville occasionally did a heavy job for Florence, like lighting the copper. They would always take in bread or meat if we were out when they were delivered. The Nevilles were very quiet neighbours, indeed we hardly noticed them as being only a lath and plaster wall away. The Chenerys ran the Shearers Arms which was nearly opposite, and Florence was on good terms with the adults, but we formed an early and firm dislike for Teddy Chenery, who was probably about my age. We thought him greedy and acquisitive if not actually a thief, and he was a well-known tell-tale who complained to his mum in a loud whine the moment he failed to get his own way on anything. We knew the Havertons at the farm but not at all well: they had rather little to do with the villagers, and in our rare encounters during this early period they made me feel a bit uncomfortable. This was mainly because I didn't know how to take them; I was not used to a relationship which seemed to require forelock-touching, or nearly. No one else lived near enough to be regularly associated with us, except for Frankie Southgate.

Frankie lived a few hundred yards from us in Owslebury Bottom, in a brick and tile cottage, one of a pair at right angles to the road, backed by the huge beeches of Jackman's Hill. He was a man with varied practical interests, and the end of his garden nearest to his house was occupied by an array of untidy and chaotic little outbuildings. A disused brick washhouse held a collection, which fascinated me, of traps and nooses of various kinds for catching animals and birds. Another shed was full of timber of all shapes and sizes, both new and decayed, as well as kindling wood – he was a devoted collector of unwanted trifles. Wooden and corrugated lean-tos held seed potatoes, coal, chicken food, vegetables stored for the winter. These little structures were all dark and alarmingly spidery on the rare occasions when I looked inside. Seen down the slope from our Medder their skyline against the beeches made them into a sort of little confused village of their own, an impression intensified by the brick chimney of the ex-washhouse. They were linked by very narrow cinder paths, and Frankie, when he wasn't out or gardening, was always to be found in one of them, and his wife usually had to shout for him when we called at the cottage door.

He was a 'roadman', and in our area this meant that he did mainly hedging and ditching. He also did quite a bit of trapping and ferreting for rabbits; we suspected he sometimes poached other game, and this was Florence's reason for politely refusing the offer of a brace of pheasants at Christmas time. He grew fine onions in his scrappy but extensive garden, and roped them properly for the winter; he forced early rhubarb in one of his many sheds and we got some pale pink tender sticks long before ours were ready; he stored carrots and turnips in earth or sand and would sometimes bring a handful of each. He knew about blackbird and pigeon pie, neither of which we fancied, and he could always be relied on to know where to get day-old chicks or a discarded wheel to replace a busted one on a barrow. We seldom met his wife, as she kept very closely to home; certainly she never once came to our cottage. She was a bent, thin, prematurely old woman who wore a fag all the time in the corner of her mouth, which caused a permanent pucker and a faint orange stain on one side of her face; her windward eye was always half-closed against the smoke. There was a sniffy-nosed little daughter called Dotty Southgate, younger than Joan or I – she must have gone to our school, but I don't remember how she got there and she didn't seem ever to be with us. On Saturdays she would sweep the little brick path which fronted her father's cottage, and her only distinction in our eyes was her pronunciation of 'bricks' when she shouted proudly over the fence, 'I swep Mummy's britches this morning!' This became a bit of family lore, often repeated.

Frankie formed a close attachment to our family – I now suspect, especially for Florence – but being an inveterate countryman he never came inside the house. A call from Frankie had an unvarying element of ritual. He always knocked on the back door, but then, surprisingly, opened it immediately, and always brought something, often an armful of neatly bundled hedge-clippings. He put his offerings on the doorstep, took off his hat, apparently to scratch his head, and then put it back on, a sceptical smile on his face as he made his standard unchanging greeting: 'I said ow *are* yer?' Though half bald, he was an impressively hairy man, his narrow face decorated with hair on all available surfaces. He shaved probably once a week, so he usually had a good stubble, but he also had owl-like growths of long hair on his upper cheek-bones almost to his eyes, hair sprouting from his ears and nostrils, and – a source of fascination to me – a collection of longish grey hairs on the bulb of his nose. The pepper and salt hairs contrasted strongly with the perpetually fresh complexion of a roadman, and with the small thread-veins across his cheeks. Even if he accepted a cup of tea, or once in a while a glass of beer, he never put a foot inside. I enjoyed his visits, which made us feel very much an organic part of Owslebury Bottom. I don't think he could read or write but he had one literary joke – his version of the address we shared – 'Owslebury Bottom, Near Winchester, Hants', which in his version became 'Owslebury's Bottom, near Winchester's pants'. This we considered a trifle improper, but ingenious.

In France, Arthur had been enduring the chaos and horror of trench warfare, interspersed with periods of illness. He was ultimately discharged in October, just before the war ended, with a tiny pension for TB after a long period of hospitalisation at Etretat, where he painted murals on the hospital walls. The word, Eight-re-ta, seemed to me to end inappropriately with 'thank you'. When he arrived at Winchester station after his discharge Florence saw that he had raised a moustache, and her opening words to him were 'Take that damn thing off!' At this time his hair was pale ginger and he parted it in the middle in common with so many of his generation. He had a large puckered scar on his neck where his tubercular glands had been operated on; and his face in repose always seemed to have an authoritarian expression as if he was being photographed with a slow exposure. After a short period of leave, most of which Arthur spent looking for a job, we saw rather little of him, as he worked in London from Monday to Friday and stayed with us only for weekends and holidays.

Almost all my life up to that November had been lived in wartime. Although I occasionally heard snatches of adult conversation about bombs, dog fights and the sinking of a German battleship, this didn't disturb my familiar daily world. I had always known that my mother's only brother had been 'killed in action', and now, learning that Frankie Southgate had 'lorst two brothers in Mespot' produced no picture of a general and overwhelming disaster. My father had difficulty in stretching his arm upwards and his flaring pink puckered scar was noticeable, but I didn't remember what he had been like before, so it was all just part of Arthur. He never talked about his experiences in the trenches in our presence. I wonder now how many bad dreams he had. There was of course no television or radio, and if newspapers came to the village, which they must have done, I never saw them. So the coming of peace made little difference to my way of life.

The immediate surroundings of the cottage had quickly become familiar to me: the Medder when I was very young, the Shearers Arms nearly opposite, and Frankie Southgate's cottage down the road. I also got to know the village – Owslebury Top – from shopping there with Florence or Joan, and from going to school and to church. There was little of purely physical beauty about the village. Most of its houses bordered the main road, and others were dotted along apparently casual stumps of lanes which led to nowhere in particular and turned quickly into footpaths or farm tracks. There was no unity of building materials: square high-shouldered brick houses of the early part of the century stood cheek by jowl with eighteenth-century lath and plaster thatched cottages; Mr Cobb's shop was frankly modern, with purplish-red brick and mustard-yellow stone facings. Many houses and farm buildings were built chiefly of flints with brickwork at the corners and edges. There were plenty of wooden shacks in people's gardens, for tools or stores or jakes, and corrugated iron roofs of an obtrusive rusty red on many a lean-to and barn. Even in the middle of the village, cow byres and stabling and muddy farmyards could just as well be in front of the houses or alongside them, as behind. A collection of similar and fairly comely white-washed houses beyond the school at Owslebury Top was punctuated by dusty or muddy yards which came right to the road; instead of hedges they had a five-barred gate and a low brick and flint wall with convex coping stones and yellow lichen and weedy grass along the top. The Ship Inn at the far end of the village was handsome in a picture-postcard sort of way, but the Shearers Arms was built with crude brick and gravy-brown woodwork. From the moment you came out of the steep tunnel of beech trees on Jackman's Hill to the beginning of Owslebury Bottom, until you left the sprawling village beyond Marwell Court, your eye did not easily escape from some evidence of squalor, neglect, or mere scruffiness.

Yet the place was beautiful to me – perhaps because all my ideas of beauty were derived from this one locality. The accumulated associations with particular corners or patches of the cottage and its surroundings merely illustrated the process of getting to love by getting to know. Three scrubby and wind-battered hawthorns that punctuated a rough hedge dividing the field beyond the Medder from the mysterious dry badlands beyond, seemed to carry for me a heavy burden of symbolic meaning, which I never quite understood. I only knew that I would see them at dawn from my bedroom window, white with blossom at Whitsun, or gaunt and brave in snow in February, and that they 'meant' the cottage and the place. At school in the middle of hearing a story read aloud, or waiting with Florence on Winchester station for the panting black London train to draw in, I would remember, and remember seeing, my three trees.

Occasionally we called at Frankie Southgate's house for something, and at least once we stayed while he and my parents talked until long after dark. By this time I was asleep. I dimly remember being lifted and a scarf being put round my neck, but the vivid memory is of waking up in my father's arms, for a moment, and seeing very clearly a wet road with its tracks or wheelmarks making a curve upwards back to the cottage; a cold, half-full moon riding alone in the sky; black bunshaped trees at the side of the road; a ragged pale skim-milk patch of cloud picking up cream colour from the moon above it. The road itself was half indigo, half azure, curving away to the little white gate and the brick path and the sitting-room with its faint familiar smell of paraffin as I half woke in the changed temperature. I was propped and carried up the narrow stairway to the low-eaved bedroom and undressed, my boots and clothes dragging on the coverlet, the nightshirt wriggled over my shoulders while whispering parents pulled back the bedclothes and let me fall sprawling inside the sheets. A momentary glance out of the uncurtained window showed me the same cold riding half-moon, the ragged cloud now sunk to a slanting patch on the horizon, and the three thorn trees guarding the skyline as I fell asleep.

Another and less cosy mystery concerned an area visible from our bedroom window. It lay beyond a little green house which was built of painted corrugated iron on a wooden frame, and seemed to embody something romantic and unattainable, on the edge of consciousness and understanding. There was nothing tangibly special about the scrubby sloping field, alongside which the flinty path ran, except that it was about as far as one could see detail, and we told one another stories about it: from the cottage it seemed hazy, misted, an area utterly remote from the friendly familiarity of the rest of the landscape. It was christened by us the Field of the Runcible Cow; the name must have come from Edward Lear, but I don't know and can't remember anything special about cows being there. Beyond this, still dimmer and mistier, was an area of chalky outcrop patched with may-bushes, privets and elders, which seemed unreachably distant, strange, quietly menacing. My eye would drop from scanning this hillside to our own dear Medder, where every yard had been walked over or rolled on.

This most incommunicable of all sensations, the poignancy or excitement or peace that the most featureless high scrubby field or broken hedge or back gate in the ivy or ridged stile can evoke, are probably the most powerful of the memories of childhood, and can shrink me in a moment to the small boy with his vague and yet powerful aspirations, like a forgotten smell that creates in one whiff a whole landscape, or some ephemeral snatch of song.

Whatever imponderables fringed it, this place was home, and the farther I wandered into the woods and fields, the more important was the anchor of the cottage and the family. We spent little time in the cottage during the fine weather, but it was always there, and following the long hot summer days were the evenings in the tiny sitting-room, and the peak points of the weekends when my father was home from his work in London.

CHAPTER THREE

FAMILY AND FRIENDS

Arthur probably had a rather lonely life in London, certainly a hard-working one, though at one stage he got addicted to playing chess at lunch-time. He lodged near the city and saw little of his parents who were still some way out in Dulwich. His weekends must have made a very strong contrast to his working week, and he concentrated a lot of activity in the precious days with his family. He found time, though, for some involvement in the village: he played cricket for the Owslebury team on Saturday afternoons, and rather fancied himself as a stylish bat and a quick field at square leg. Another member of the cricket team was Stan Hutchins, the postman. His regular method of delivering letters, always very early in the morning, was to ring his bicycle bell, walk up the path and hand up the letters to Florence or Arthur who could just reach them by leaning out of the bedroom window. In the cricket season he and Arthur would make cheerful arrangements and comments about the coming match, or look forward to the batting of Will Williams, the policeman, who on a good day would slog the ball several times for a boundary. White flannels were *de rigueur*, and Arthur's pair were thick creamy white and so tight that Florence always feared they would split down the back when he stooped for a low ball or sneaked a single: as far as I know they never did.

He also wrote, directed and painted the scenery for a play, which was performed in the village hall in aid of the Cricket Club funds. I remember clearly the thirty pages or so of the script being written in longhand in special ink and pressed on to the stiff yellow jelly contained in a flat tin like a cooking tin – a piece of apparatus the manufacturers marketed as a Hectograph, but which we always called the Jellygraph. This produced twenty or so copies for the cast; we helped to manufacture these with an attractive little wooden roller, and they came out with pale violet letters on shiny white paper, easily crumpled. Arthur painted the scenery in sections in our barn and assembled them in the village hall – an exquisite sunny garden scene, I thought, with towering spires of bright perennials and a sundial, lawns, a blue sky with fish-shaped clouds, all seen through French windows. One of the daughters of Mr Haverton played a leading party and I still remember her sitting in a deckchair on the stage, to my eye the essence of adult sophistication – the sleeveless dress, the flat and featureless chest, the waist nearly crossing the pelvis, short skirts, long legs, strapped shoes, dark shingled hair making twin commas across the cheeks, and an immensely long cigarette holder. The play itself, the first I had ever seen, evoked a world of lovely colour and polish, though the only fragment of script that remains was the declaration of the comic hero in a striped blazer, who went in for spoonerisms and said 'I pove Loppy' – carefully explained to me as his version of 'I love Poppy'. I sat in the middle of the hall which was hot, smoky and airless, in curious contrast to the splendidly romantic and wildly funny goings-on on the stage. In the interval there were huge quantities of bottled beer served from side tables. Florence played the interval music, including a lot of her 'pieces', before she vanished behind the curtains to prompt the second half. At the end shouts and screams for 'Author' and 'Producer' went on for a long time, but were finally satisfied when my father, looking small and flushed, appeared on stage, wildly clapped not only by the audience but by all the actors. At last we left the familiar parish hall, usually a rather startling cream and dark green but, as we left in the dark, looking black and large with orange windows. We walked home in the starlight, Joan and I dozy but elated, and very proud of our talented father.

The vision of Arthur, small but proud, being fêted by the whole cast of his play has stayed with me. Although he was only five foot seven, he considered himself a good height. 'You needn't worry, old man,' he said to me when people commended me for growing (he called me 'old man' from the age of four) 'so long as you grow up to be my height.' He was a person of repeated catch-phrases. Joan, fiercely loyal in most things, imitated him till Bill and I learned to use his tags ironically when he was out of earshot. The phrases coloured our lives, and to hear them now or even think of them brings that remote life sharply back. When we wandered around the room he would always say, 'Bring yourself to an anchor.' If we had a small punch-up indoors he always objected with the same phrase – 'If you children want to bearsark go into the garden': 'bearsark' was a life-long verb for him and only decades later was I able to trace it to the Boer War 'going berserk': even now I tend to think of it as a verb. We all liked boiled sweets, and Arthur would say, perfectly seriously as he held out the paper packet, 'Have an acidulated drop': I think he thought 'acid drop' a bit vulgar. When he wanted to challenge someone's statement, especially about himself, he would say 'I like that!' meaning – and I found this most confusing – 'I don't like that at all.' Other favourites were: 'The man's an absolute shyster'; 'Treat him (her, it) with contumely' (at one stage I thought this was a kind of ointment, like 'Treat it with Zam-buk'); 'You might have the common decency to think of others'; 'He was only chi-iking' (kidding). 'You can be rude to me if you must, but I will not have you being rude to your mother' – 'Your Mother', in gothic letters, seemed a different person from Florence. If we said 'I love blackberries' or 'I love hazel-nut creams,' he would be certain to say 'You cannot love an inanimate object.' He was prone to labelling people with tags which I then took to be amiable descriptions and only much later thought of as prejudiced – 'Ikey mo', 'A touch of the tarbrush', 'A real gentleman'. He always spoke of 'a sovereign' and 'half a sovereign' instead of a quid or ten bob. The whole family, for reasons which are still unclear, said 'threadled' instead of 'threaded', and 'spreadled' instead of 'spreaded', or, indeed, 'spread', so that we busily 'threadled' needles and 'spreadled' grain for the chickens: whether Arthur was responsible for this aberration I don't know.

Arthur took himself pretty seriously. He always meant well and thought of himself as very very special – better spoken, better educated, democratic only from a great height, and above all, just about to become a leading business man and make a great deal of money – 'not for myself of course, but for you children and your mother. I'm not in the least interested in money.'

Florence, too, was proud of her background, and sometimes dragged details of her father's money and cousin's education into the conversation, but this was done with a kind of innocence and naïvety, and she always mocked and ridiculed snobbery – 'He's putting it on!' 'Airs and graces!' 'She thinks a lot of herself!' 'What a swankpot!' I don't think she ever thought of herself as superior to any village people. She still had traces of her mother's American accent. From her I caught a tendency to say 'can' instead of 'tin', 'horrizon', a much more shadowy and beautiful word than the prosaic and wooden 'horighson', and 'clemaytis' instead of 'clematis'. Joan and I often looked at Florence's and Arthur's wedding photograph, which was permanently displayed on the chest of drawers in their bedroom. It was in sepia, the thick white surround slightly embossed, with the name of the Dulwich photographer in brown italics. Arthur was wearing a very high winged collar nearly up to the lobes of his ears, and Florence's collar was equally high and close-fitting, part of her white waisted dress with leg-of-mutton sleeves; she had a circlet of flowers in her hair as well as a bunch of lilies-of-the-valley at her waist. She looked pleased and reasonably at ease, but Arthur had a stern expression and was turned slightly from the camera. We wondered (the malicious suggestion was originally Joan's) if he was standing on a box, as the crowns of the newly married couple's heads were exactly level.

My mother seemed to me to look quite different from the other women in Owslebury. She was short-skirted and slender, with hands and feet conspicuously long and narrow. Her thin hands ended in ridgy nails which she claimed indicated a hereditary tendency to rheumatism: her left wrist had a crescent-shaped scar which fascinated us, and she wore lots of rings and bracelets, all loose because of her thin bones, and therefore dropped into the washing up, lost in the chicken mash, left in the village shop, even once disappearing into our home-made cesspit, but somehow always recovered after plenty of agitation and drama. She was fashionably flat-chested, indeed in round-necked dresses showed pronounced salt-cellars. Her dark brown hair was not hairpinned up into a tight bun but cut short so that it floated free as she dashed about. Even as early as this, while she was yet in her twenties, it was greying rapidly, and this looked excitingly incongruous with the smooth unlined youth of her skin. Her eyes were between grey and hazel, and they had the very faintest cast, seldom noticeable face to face but often apparent in photographs.

Florence sang round the house in a good clear mezzo-soprano. She had quite a repertoire of songs and in the absence of a piano sang unaccompanied to entertain the family, sometimes with Joan and later with the rest of us. Among them at one end were several of the Schubert *lieder*, and at the other *Indian Love Lyrics, Down in the Forest, Curly-Headed Babby* (a mock Negro spiritual), *A Brown Bird Singing*, and an amazing set of five songs about marital loss and parting:

> I have lighted the logs in my ingle nook
> To serve as the wanderer's guide,

and later the revelation that

> My beacon flame is calling by name
> The wanderer through the snow

I felt this latter to be deeply moving and early thought of it as embodying both the trials and splendours of being grown up.

More incredible and more memorable (I've not seen the words since) was another of the five songs, called *The Night Nursery*.

> When nurse has put the candle out
> And stumped across the floor
> She says that not a single soul
> Must come inside the door;
> There's only me and Mick the dog
> What sleeps along o' me
> Knows why the skylight opens
> And what we're going to see.
>
> For when the sun has gone away
> The world is put to bed,
> There's someone comes to see me then

Who Nursie says is dead.
Dad used to call her 'Darling heart!'
But Muvver was her name,
And Mick and me were very sad
Before our Muvver came.

She comes in through the window
'Cos the door is not allowed;
Her eyes are like the shining stars
Her hair is like a cloud.
She holds me very close to her
And talks about a land
Where all the flowers are boys and girls
With mothers close at hand.

And when I want to go with her
She says t'would never do –
''Cos Daddy would be lonely, son
Without a man like you.'

Although I couldn't identify totally with the boy narrator of this frequently sung piece, as he was of the class to have an old nurse to himself, I shared his main anguish and the thought of a whole life with his Daddy, tolerable in itself, but intolerable if his mother – I knew who it was with hair 'like a cloud' – was going to fade away by dawn. Tears filled my eyes, easy but irresistible tears, every time this ballad was sung.

I thought Florence beautiful, and everyone in the village seemed to like her; she was permissive and comfortable by contrast with the high-principled Arthur. I think she suffered patches of depression or worry – 'I've got the hump today,' or from Joan, 'Mummy has one of her headaches' – the word 'migraine' was unknown – but her attitude to life in general was that it was, or should be, cosy, with a strong coloured thread of humour. She was never demonstrative ('Don't be sloppy' came quite early into her bits of advice to us), but was deeply affectionate; we all understood this very early on, and a sigh or a slight watering of the eyes from her seemed more significant than tantrums or floods of tears from others.

Nothing could get her down for long, at least not in those days, and she faced some years of relative poverty with great courage and adaptability. I never once heard her complain to Arthur about his money failures or his delusions of tycoonish grandeur. It couldn't have been easy for her, I now realise, being alone for five days a week with three children, the oldest of us six when we arrived in Owslebury. She was a rotten cook and knew it: she was rueful and sometimes a bit tearful about this, but often managed to turn her failures into comedy. Still, she made some splendid things like bread pudding, roly-poly pudding and vast stews, though her relatively privileged upbringing had perhaps ill prepared her for coping with a copper. A sample of her bravery occurred when she cut open the breast of a laying White Leghorn pullet which was cropbound; she was concerned for the chicken's survival as well as its egg production. She was wincing and swallowing as she made the wavering cut, emptied the smelly contents of the crop and then sewed it up with a needle and thread; we all cheered when it ran off apparently none the worse for the experience. It was Florence who thought the fetlocks of our old horse Jo were untidy and trimmed them with scissors, getting for thanks a nasty kick in the thigh which stayed yellow and purple for weeks.

One of her few fears was of spiders, a fear which Arthur shared but tried to conceal, and I caught this from her early on, in spite of several attempts to train myself out of it, starting with money spiders, and working up. The thatch of the cottage encouraged huge house-spiders, and it was doubtful whether most terror was inspired by one of these little monsters scampering across the living-room floor and seen out of the corner of the eye, or by a stationary large black one spreadeagled on a bedroom wall or ceiling. Both produced immense tension and crisis. Even in midwinter a window was opened wide when we spotted a mural spider; it was coaxed to cling to the head of a broom, which was then tapped violently on the sill, with plenty of accompanying shudders and vocal tremolos. The ones that had the impertinence to cross the floor – where they darted for cover with extraordinary speed – were eventually cornered, and stamped into the floor bricks with a violence and heel-grinding which mashed their surprisingly impalpable bodies into nothing. So shrieks upstairs never meant that the curtains were on fire or the ceiling down – merely that a spider had been sighted.

Most days Joan and I got home fairly promptly from school, partly because her very high sense of duty made her keen not to keep Florence waiting to hear the news that we were both well, unstabbed by projecting thorns, ungored by bulls, unkidnapped by the 'Owslebury and district gangsters'. To this end she often tugged me away from afternoon playground games; once in a while, though, we paid a call for Florence after school. One afternoon in early spring – it must have been my first spring at school – we set off in an unfamiliar direction past the church to collect some wool from Mrs Jefferies who lived in a thatched cottage next door to Granny Baker's shop. The family included a daughter of Joan's age, and while they talked together her brother, Jimmy, two years older than I and not therefore a close friend, invited me into his enviable one-man bedroom to see his birds' eggs. I was instantly entranced by these exquisite objects lying in silver sand, each of which he solemnly named.

'My bestun is that there kingfisher but at's bruk on the underside.'

He showed me. Vistas opened up instantly, and when he gave me, wrapped in cotton-wool, three of his swaps, a blackbird's, a hedge sparrow's, and a magpie's, I had already decided that I would start my own collection.

'Magpies is common but hard to git, in a prickly nest wiv a kinda roof on it. They allus build up a prickly tree,' he explained.

'This ere's a good time to start – March – April – May is best. Tellyerwot, you find a nest and only take one egg, and I'll show you at school ow to blow em – quite easy when you get the knack.'

At first my search for nests and their delectable contents was restricted to the small area round the cottage, though Joan started helping me on the way back from shcool. I quickly became totally single-minded about eggs and no journey was free from at least a little peering into hedges or along verges. I didn't go far afield: for one thing I might meet Ernie Bone.

Every society includes a figure of menace, alien and fearsome, unlike the rest of us. Ernie Bone played this part in our village; he turned up without announcement, meshed briefly with our lives and then vanished equally suddenly, reabsorbed into the landscape as he pushed on to Cheriton or Bishop's Waltham. He was my childhood version of this archetype – the scapegoat and bogyman upon which all one's nervy-sniggering childhood fears could settle.

I now suspect that Ernie was some sort of war casualty, probably suffering from shellshock or war neurosis. He was a tramp, and seemed immensely old, but was perhaps in his forties, though ill-preserved by poverty and madness. He had a grizzled beard, hair which was notably long for this very shorn period of our history, and eyes so bloodshot that the whites were not white at all but a smoother continuation of the weather-reddened cheeks. Summer and winter he wore an army greatcoat over an assortment of dustbin clothes. His trousers, coat and boots were tied up with twine – whiskery yellowish twine of the kind used by reapers and binders, which he presumably picked up in the farmyards and roadways. His hairy ears were grimed with filth and his neck mapped with creased black lines; his hands had claw-like nails, long and untrimmed like his hair, and of an inky blackness. He stank abominably. His possessions were in an army haversack and a hessian bag worn round his neck and tied, again, with binder twine. He was tall, thin and bent: his voice, when he was being civil or whining, was low and creaking like a rusted lock; but when angry, and nearly always when speaking to children, he shouted through his dribbly beard in what was to us a terrifying roar. He scrounged his way from village to village, battening on to people's kindness and pity if they were well-disposed, and frightening the wits out of the solitary or elderly or nervous.

He had the unnerving habit of sleeping in our barn without asking. On a dark frosty morning in winter, a trip to the barn to get chicken food or a chopper if the fire had gone out was always accompanied by a chilling fear that Ernie might emerge from the straw and rubbish in the corner, himself an animated bundle of rubbish, and shout at me – or worse, whisper something horrid. He always begged for food and money, but would never come, as far as I knew, into anyone's house. He certainly never came into ours, though once my father quixotically invited him in. Mercifully Ernie refused, and stayed, like Frankie Southgate, on the back doorstep. He didn't seem to care for beer and drank only spirits, though at our back door he would down several cups of unusually sweet tea ('More sugar, missus' he would say, as my mother piled in the heaped teaspoons) and left fingerprints and smudgy mouth-prints on the cup's rim.

Mr Toombs, whose Christian name I never knew, was an infrequent visitor who turned up perhaps half a dozen times a year – never by arrangement, always as a surprise. He had first met my father in the army hospital at Etretat. He travelled over a wide area of Hampshire selling wholesale groceries, and owned what we considered an impressive motor van, usually packed to the roof top with cartons and boxes so that only the driver's seat was free and even that was in danger of invasion. The van was black and had a running board on each side, the metal tread of which was always spotless, like the polished curved brass of the radiator top and the brass front lamps. Once Mr Toombs took my mother for a drive in it; this involved humping box after box of groceries into the cottage to make room for her to sit down by the driver. I had the childish impression that he – and indeed other male visitors of the period – rather fancied Florence. Certainly it seemed to me, standing guard over the groceries in the cottage and lifting a cardboard corner to peek at tins and packets, that they were a long time 'going for a spin'. On the other hand, Mr Toombs looked so funny that I can't now believe for a moment that his sentiments, if he had any, could have been returned by Florence. He had a long, sad, toothy face with a lantern jaw; his skull was small and his dark hair was neatly plastered down to it. His mouth, lips, teeth and jaw all seemed huge and when, fifteen years later, I first saw the French actor Fernandel it was not only with pleasure but with recognition: he was exactly like Mr Toombs. I loved him. Close up he smelt strongly of newly baked bread. His hands were like his jaw; wrists, palms, fingers and nails hugely extended and inhumanly clean – so big that they looked unmanageable. Those hands were always active, and made our tea cups and saucers look like those of a doll's house tea-set.

He was always full of news of the area. I first heard the word 'Basingstoke' from his lips, and he spoke familiarly of Christchurch and Southampton and even Portsmouth: this gave him glamour, and I pictured him as living in a perpetual excitement of visiting new places. Whatever direction the dialogue took, he was always reminded at frequent intervals of something he had in the back of the van, and walked several times along the brick path, often tailed by me, to unlock its back doors and rummage for anything from a tin of jelly sweets to a packet of nightlights. These were pressed on us in addition to the presents with which he arrived, so that the sitting-room took on the look of the village shop by the time he left, and Florence would say, 'Oh Pete, he really shouldn't!' I remember his giving us a little blue package produced by Boots Cash Chemists and called 'Boots Pocket Ambulance Case'. It contained tightly rolled bandages, ointments, emollient creams and even a pair of tweezers for taking out splinters, all much too neatly packed ever to be used. Several things specially delighted me – saws, hammers, planes and screwdrivers made of chocolate, and tissue packets of tinny little toys. All of us enjoyed Mr Toombs' visits, and we three children felt a sensation of social pleasure combined with satisfied greed. He drank tea, tea by the bucketful – a remarkable sight, as he seldom stayed long.

When we returned from a walk we were thrilled if we saw the black van with its two unwinking carriage-lamps outside the cottage, occupying a dangerous width of the tiny road; we knew then that we were in for more bready kisses and gifts on a scale that reminded us of Christmas morning. Like Ernie Bone, Mr Toombs flitted in and out of our lives incalculably; Ernie was the menace who crept in unannounced, and Mr Toombs appeared, equally unheralded, a beloved Greek bearing gifts.

CHAPTER FOUR

THE MEDDER STORES

At this time we had enough money to accumulate a supporting cast of people and animals. A girl called Hilda Jewkes, in her late teens, scatty, gossipy, soft, helped in the house as well as taking us children out during the holidays. One of a large family in the village, Tim Hunney, blond, brown and strong, worked in the garden. White Leghorns and Buff Orpingtons roamed the Medder. They looked from the bedroom window like piles of feathers or dry beech leaves or horsechestnut petals blown on water. The cocks crowed through the misty dawns of summer. The birds were enclosed at night, but by day they ranged over the whole Medder, and they became a flock only when they were fed; then they ran like footballers through the grass at Florence's loud clucking or at the banging of a wooden spoon on their mash bucket. We had a lot of chickens; at one time Joan counted a hundred, but this included day-old chicks, cockerels and pensioners. At intervals some got out of their ramshackle enclosure and insisted on roosting in the leggy hawthorns. Occasionally a fox or stoat would get one, and we would find grisly remains and a sad pile of tail feathers with bloodstained quills. When the unenclosed field beyond was reaped after a crop of oats or wheat, the chickens were run on it. They sometimes laid in the boxes we provided for them, but also pretty often in the long grass under the hawthorns, and once Bill, when he was playing on his own by the garden hedge, found a nest of fifteen. Unfortunately they were already addled.

Then there was Joe, the old and very lazy horse. He pulled a two-wheeled cart for us, at least when the road was flat or downhill. When faced by an uphill stretch he behaved more like a donkey or a mule and just stopped, cropping the roadside grass if he could reach. If you got out and led him by the reins he would go slowly and pantingly up to the top. As we lived in a valley this problem arose rather often. Tim and Joe took me a couple of times into Winchester, I think to get sacks of porridge oats, chicken meal and seed potatoes, though I was more fascinated by the eight miles return journey than the shopping. I sat up on the board with Tim, who put a sack to stop the ribbing of the cart from catching the small of my back. He let me take the reins on quiet stretches through the cool shadows of trees and out in the blazing sunshine where the road dipped sharply and the bank up into the adjoining field made dazzlingly white little chalk cliffs. Joe was usually sluggish to the point of immobility, so we were doubly delighted when the rare sound of a hunting horn awoke in him old memories and he actually reared and pranced in the Medder.

We had an attractive brown-and-white mongrel dog called Bunty, whom we all loved dearly and regarded as one of the family, though at intervals he was wicked in a way which strained our powers of forgiveness. One winter evening Florence had proudly displayed to a visitor three blue jerseys identical but for size, the last of which she had just finished knitting, and then unwisely left on the settee. Between candle-out and dawn Bunty pulled them to pieces, and the loss of the jerseys was more endurable than Florence's tears.

Although he was a bit of a wood-butcher, Arthur was clever-fingered and ingenious and he made lots of gadgets for the house and garden. He acquired a heavy marble slab, about four-feet long, and because he firmly believed that a cold surface was essential for pastry-making and other domestic processes, he managed to jam this slab between the spindly legs of an upside-down table: since we always referred to the cottage kitchen as 'the scullery' this was called the scullery table. It groaned a little under its own weight, and crumbs and other detritus tended to lodge inside the wooden ledges of the bottom – that is, the top; these ledges couldn't be removed as they alone provided sufficient tensile strength to keep the supporting legs in their relatively upright position, and they were a hazard for one's toes at meal times. All the food preparation, cooking, washing up, flower arranging, shoe-mending and most of the meals, except in the coldest months when we ate in the sitting-room, took place on this astonishing contraption (though it seems so utterly familiar that I only realise how astonishing it was when I come to write it down). We were fond of the table and proud of our ingenious father.

Most memorably Arthur built us the hut on the Medder. He put it up one warm holiday morning, with me 'helping', while Florence was doing the washing. We started by carrying out four big posts from the barn. I could just manage to lift my end, and Arthur wouldn't let me help him drag them up the steep earth steps. 'Leave this to me, old man,' he said, and red with exertion, he pulled the first one up on to the dewy grass. 'Now perhaps you can assist again, Peter.' I was proud to do so.

When we got the posts to the site he gave me the first of a series of orders.

'Will you go back to the scullery to ask your mother to give you the big chopper? It's probably in the usual place by the copper.'

'And, Peter,' he shouted after me, 'you are not to run with it. It's exceedingly sharp, and I don't want you to hurt yourself.'

By the time I got back he had started digging the first hole, and he managed to make a kind of rough point to one end of the post with the chopper while I held the other end.

'Endeavour to hold it steady, Peter, but be careful of the nails.'

'Would you be so kind as to get the chair from the barn?'

I carried the not-very-secure wooden chair across the garden and with some difficulty up into the Medder. Arthur stood on it and, holding Frankie Southgate's sledge-hammer, which I could only just lift, he managed to bang the post in a foot or so, while I held it and felt the tremors right up to my armpits. Then we had to get the two bits of sheet galvanised iron which, with his inveterate acquisitiveness, he had at some time begged from a heap of discards at the back of someone's barn. They were past their best, rusty at the edges and pockmarked. We found them difficult to carry, and the slight breeze made my end feel as though it was about to take off and me with it. Still, we managed them, half dragged, half carried, across the grass. Arthur declined to tell me exactly how the hut was to be constructed: perhaps he wasn't sure himself. He measured the short side against the erected post and put me as a marker while he got the spade and dug a second hole. The comedy of the chair, the sledge-hammer, the tremors, the projecting three-inch nails was gone through again. Finally, we got the four posts in, forming a square, and felt we had earned a cup of tea, though Florence was less than elated when required to stop washing and make it from the black kettle which sat all day on the fire.

The next stage was to hump the cross-members, and some of them had to be sawn to fit. As I held the end of the wood resting across the chair and Arthur sawed away, there was the most appalling screech, but it was only after several more strokes that he reluctantly discarded the view that it was a knot in the wood, and decided he was sawing on a nail. He looked at me.

'I regret asking you to undertake so many errands, Peter. Your mother is unlikely to be amused by another interruption, but a prophet is not without honour save in his own country. Please ask her for the pincers from the drawer – not the pliers, the pincers.'

When I arrived in the cool scullery with its shaft of sunlight bisecting my mother, she was wet to the elbows with the washing, but dried her hands and arms before she found the pincers which were on a high shelf and not in the drawer at all. 'Your father!' was all she actually said, but she gave me a quick hug at the same time, perhaps to break up the male trade union.

When I got back to the Medder, Arthur was rolling a cigarette, and the wispy yellow tobacco blew in the light breeze. So I stood on the chair and held my jacket round his head while he lit up at the second attempt. After a few drags he put the damp cigarette aside and finished sawing. Then he found he needed nails, which both of us had forgotten.

'At least you won't have to go into the scullery again, old man,' said Arthur with a smile.

'We shall need the big ones in the tin near the window. I'm sorry to be so forgetful.'

Only a momentary reluctance to pick up a tin which might be spidery delayed me, and I ran back across the grass, accompanied this time by Bunty, to find that Arthur had managed to light up again and was smoking cheerfully. He knocked the nails sideways into the cross-members and then shook the whole framework proudly to show how firm it was. We bent one piece of galvanised iron over the whole structure to form straight sides and a curved roof: Arthur made a long nick with the spade, buried six inches of the metal and then nailed it on the timber frame, finishing by burying the other end in another slot in the turf. I was delighted to be allowed to help with the nailing of the iron, and if some of my nails went crooked and had to be bashed flat, they still helped to hold the metal in place. Finally, we put the second sheet in place to act as a back to the building and nailed it easily to the now firm and secure 'hut'. It projected some way into the air as we had nothing to cut sheet metal with, but that didn't seem in any way a disadvantage. The front was open to the wind and weather. After the last nail was driven in, we called the whole family out to admire it, and Florence was clearly proud of her inventive, if slightly scatty husband. She hugged me and we were taken back in modest triumph to the cottage, where we had another of our interminable cups of tea – this one made specially in honour of the male warriors returned from the wars. And very soon after this we had a huge meal made of bits and pieces left over from our Sunday dinner; it went down extremely well after our hard morning's labouring.

When we went out to look at it after lunch, we found that the puckered nail holes which dotted the metal made small spangles of sunlight inside the hut. We spent many happy hours in this odd structure. Joan and I fixed it up as a shop with a counter, and labelled it in chalk *The Medder Stores*, and though you couldn't have shelves fastened to metal, you could rest some of your display on the quite heavy timbers, also pitted with nail holes, which helped to hold the whole thing up. We pestered Florence to keep tea packets, matchboxes, the blue sugar bags, which we filled with dock seed, even fag-paper containers – anything one could get a 'run' of – and stacked them meticulously with price labels and rejected showcards of Arthur's to help the display. Joan was the bossy and efficient shopkeeper, and I was a series of eccentric customers, while Bill played haystacks just outside through the long hot days of summer.

Bill's haystacks were a great satisfaction to him for the

whole season; he would put four sticks in the ground to make a rectangle, pack long grasses into the space, lovingly combed so that they all lay in one direction, get Florence or Joan to help him trim the projecting ends with scissors, and finally take the sticks away. A couple of days later when the grass stems had bleached a bit they were convincing miniatures of the Havertons' haystacks, until the wind and rain scattered them or blurred their spruce shapeliness.

Later on the Medder Stores became a sitting-room, with a piano chalked on the rusty wall. I found the perspective of the keys very difficult to draw, but far easier was the pot of flowers I drew on its top, modelled on memories of our grandparents' sitting-room. We made pretend-tea out of dock seeds, in a blue enamelled teapot complete with lid but with a hole near the spout, and served it to visitors in broken cups found on, or rather in, a rubbish dump in Gough's Lane. The inside of this sitting-room got surprisingly warm. Even though one side was open to the air the metal conducted the heat, and the atmosphere was like the tea tent at the village fête – filtered light, sweaty enclosure and trampled grass.

Florence seldom left us for more than an hour or two, but once she went out for a day's visit to the Ansteys with Joan. Hilda was left to look after Bill and me for the day, so she took us, me on foot and Bill in the pushchair, to dinner with a friend of hers. Marge Bradford was married to the shepherd.

It was a sweltering day in late August, after what seemed like months of holiday. The shepherd's cottage stood by itself some way out of the village on a high bit of dry ground. Far from being charmingly old-fashioned it was improbably urban-looking with metal curlicues along the ridge and eaves, of the kind I associate with railway stations. It was of harsh red brick with gravy-coloured wood trimmings to tone, and its dry chalky front garden sported only a parched platoon of annuals panting against the brickwork.

By the time we arrived we were hot, not so much as a result of toiling up Crabbe's Hill as of the beating sun on the flat low-hedged road to Shep's house. Marge Bradford came to the door before we could knock; she was red-faced, plump, bare-armed and so fair that she seemed to have no eyebrows or eyelashes. She welcomed us in; Bill was quickly settled with his crayons, which Hilda had brought from home, and Marge launched into a quickfire and not very intelligible gossip with Hilda, about family and village acquaintances. I was sent to 'play' till dinner in the surprisingly large vegetable garden. This was completely hidden from the road by the high-shouldered house and sloped sharply downwards, getting lusher as it fell, finally, into a chaos of nettles and flowering hogweed. It was my first close-up of a really well-kept vegetable garden, and I was surprised and impressed as I moved slowly from row to row in the blinding heat. The vegetables I saw were splendid beyond belief. The straight cinder path which bisected the garden reminded me of Frankie Southgate's; it made such a contrast with our scruffy and crooked path of grass, daisies and irrepressible nettles. The rhubarb sticks, red-green and as thick as my upper arm, were topped with veined leaves like umbrellas. There were two rows of marrow plants and the marrows lay grossly among the large leaves and the star-shaped yellow flowers. They reminded me vividly of the sausage-shaped cushions, striped in yellow and green, on the *chaise-longue* in the Havertons' sitting-room. Arthur had more than once referred to this bit of furniture, and having memorised the name I now proudly repeated it to myself. Where we had one winding row of radishes, Shep Bradford had six, drawn and spaced as if with a ruler, their shoulders popping out from the soil, scarlet and uniform. The rows seemed very long, and there was not a weed to be seen in the neatly hoed lines. Runners twined up heavy poles and were weighed down with their clusters of beans, fat and very long and topped by brilliant red blossom. The beetroot grew in several long rows, each one the size of a coconut. They sat in the soil and were finished off with a great top-knot of purple foliage. The carrots were clean-looking and touched one another. They were the size of my small wrists, and their foliage made a neat but fluffy-edged rectangle of lacy green. The potatoes, row after row after row of them, were meticulously ridged up with steep slopes of soil, but an occasional white tuber was bursting through among the rich haulms smothered in mauve bloom and cabbage white butterflies. There was a forest of parsnip foliage, and tomatoes in huge swags showed every stage of ripeness from pale green to scarlet. Cos lettuces, fat, smug and uniform as soldiers, were tied with raffia, and interspersed with patches of newly raked fallow. There seemed to be none of the dead leaves, weedy patches and general messiness so familiar in our own small-scale and measly vegetable garden. I wondered a bit how Shep had time to do all this, and who managed to eat it all.

When I was called in, or rather bellowed in, for dinner, he had returned from his rounds with his two wild but shy children, tanned almost as brown as he. They were among the biguns at school and I hardly knew them to talk to. I was ushered into the kitchen-sitting-room which was strikingly lined, ceiling included, in pitchpine, all the wood varnished so that everything looked shiny and sticky. Hilda was flushed and excited, the children waiting quietly, Bill big-eyed on his large varnished chair and Shep at the head of the table. He smelt of lanolin and sheep, and sat hairy and red-faced with his knife and fork held vertically as he waited for the dinner. Marge brought to the table blue and white vegetable dishes, the first steaming and weighed down with slices of marrow looking like water-ice, the second piled with enormous floury potatoes, the third heaped with runner beans. Then there arrived the *pièce de résistance*, a meat pudding oozing steam and rich smells – enough, I would have thought, for a small army. As it was cut up it steamed still more, and each of our plates was piled high with pudding and vegetables. The shiny varnish, the red hairy face of Shep Bradford and the piles of steaming food made an unforgettable impression on my mind. I got hotter and hotter.

Second helpings were offered. I was bloated, and said, 'Thank you, but I can't eat any more.' Marge regarded this as merely a polite gesture to be brushed aside, and piled my plate up yet again. As I had been brought up never to leave food on the plate, I forced it down.

'Wanna hev plenty o' grub,' Shep advised me between mouthfuls. 'Make a man of yer – keep yer goin.'

The light in the room from the blazing sunlight outside was darker now – the curtains made it purplish, too, against the foxy red of the varnished walls which seemed to be sweating in sympathy. Plates were stacked and cleared away, and Marge carried in a huge jam roly-poly steaming up to the varnished ceiling, and from this, enormous wedges of jam-oozing steamed pudding were put on our plates. I felt torpid and foodlogged but we all tucked in manfully.

Shep, perhaps a bit redder than before, went back cheerfully to his work with his two children, slim and shy as whippets, and Hilda took Bill and me, after long and fulsome farewells and kisses from Marge, for a walk up to Mr Schwartz's forest. I clung desperately to the pushchair for the first few minutes and stumbled along, suitably scared by the black pine forests, but mainly stuffed to the eyebrows with Shep Bradford's veggies and Marge Bradford's cooking. Bill slept nearly all the way home.

We hadn't got very far when Hilda said, 'Wasn't that a lovely dinner? Marge carnarf cook, and that jam puddin, that was the best I ever hid. Sometimes they comes out a bit slimy.' This was too much for me and I said, 'Hilda, I think I'm going to be sick.'

'Go behind that hedge, then – quick, through the gap there!' While I retched into the grasses Hilda shouted, 'Oh come on, Pete, do!' and this stimulated another heave. At length I emerged and she wiped my mouth with my handkerchief.

'Now, Pete, don't tell yer mum about this – she'll never forgive me, and I tell yer what, she 'ont never let me take yer aht to dinner with the Bradfords agin. You wouln' like that now, would yer?'

Wanly I agreed, but didn't find myself at that moment keenly anticipating another meal in the varnished room. As we walked down the brick path Hilda reminded me again in a stage whisper that I wasn't to report my recent experience. So apart from some reluctance on my part to eat as much tea as usual, the evening passed normally. As I thought over the day's experiences I remembered being told that Shep reckoned he walked 'on a avridge' about twenty-five miles every day, and at last understood why his vegetable garden and Marge's meals were on such a scale.

This reminds me of another long walk in the same direction, this time with Hilda and Joan. It was October, summery but cool, and we took the pram up Crabbe's Hill and out on to the long road to Schwartz's, past Shep's house. Marge tapped on the window and waved, but we didn't stop. Hilda was telling Joan interminable, incomprehensible stories about goings-on in the village, punctuating them by pushing back her hair with one hand. Joan listened with steady attention, as she helped push the pram. I seem to remember our wearing mittens, though it wasn't yet really cold. The pram, already shabby when it was first used for Bill, was now really on its last wheels – rusty, uncertain in the brakes, peeling in the coach-work, its hood holed and worn, the framework rusted like the spokes of the wheels. Still, it was the nearest we had to a vehicle, and it was used for a variety of fairly heavy humping jobs.

Soon we went off the road and along a winding rutty track hedged with hazel and birch. I dawdled to pick the late blackberries, bright and shiny black in the sunlight, though they lacked flavour, as the devil had long spat on them. The ruts were of farm-waggon width and the much higher grassy bits between them were bumpy, so that the pram rattled and jerked and jumped. Hilda didn't seem to mind at all, as she was in full flow about the awful way the Carters exploited their lodger and made him dig their garden for nothing while he was trying to save up to marry Milly, who was beautiful but not very bright and lived in Mill Lane just as Rosie Lane lived in Rose Lane. Variations on this theme lasted until we reached the end of the track. Beyond and to our left was the forbidding mass of Schwartz's 'forest'. We thought it vast – perhaps it was a hundred acres – and I disliked it intensely for a number of reasons: it was so dark that I guessed from hurried glimpses that nothing grew inside except an occasional fern and pallid toadstool, and I knew from boys at school that there were few birds there except for the odd magpie or crow and, if you were lucky, a goldcrest somewhere on the edge. At school we firmly believed it was patrolled by savage dogs and fearful gamekeepers under the charge of the alien Schwartz with his wicked un-English ways of going on. Our destination was a little deciduous wood sloping away towards Baybridge, and always full of treasures. In one corner there were a few sweet-chestnut trees, and Joan, impetuous as always, and thinking of roasting chestnuts by the early fires we lit in the evenings, bravely extracted some nuts, but was soon jumping up and down with pricked hands. Then we thought of using a stick to beat open the hedgehog carapaces and reveal the bright polished nuts nested together inside. We had brought with us a bag, generally used for collecting hazel-nuts, and made of harsh sacking dyed crimson, blue and cream; we hung this from a projection on the pram, and put the chestnuts we collected into it. I suppose we got a couple of pounds altogether. A few were neatly bitten by squirrels or birds. Some of the fattest of the delicately ridged chestnuts were still white, but like conkers they went a matt brown before the afternoon was over, though they never acquired the glorious shine of the ripe ones. Hundreds of green hedgehogs lay unopened on top of the rich yielding layer of leaf-mould and rotting wood, tinder-dry on the top, damp just below and smelling of hay-ricks. Fungi projected like shelves from a fallen trunk; we called them Jews' Ears – 'Don't touch, Pete, they're poisonous' from the know-all Hilda, who thought all fungi except mushrooms were poisonous and even felt suspicious about them. She was wrong about this, though she was right about the fly agaric which we came upon later and found so beautiful with its red-and-white top, and about the stinkhorn, which no one presumably would ever want to eat because of its overpowering stench.

We carried armfuls of wood snapped to roughly the right size for the little pram standing in the leaves and dry bents at the copse's edge. Some of the bark was already speckled with coral spots, some little logs were almost puffy with longitudinal fibres of rotting wood loosely encased in cylinders of leathery bark, some branches were still firm and fairly hard to break. We all got hot humping and breaking up the wood, and the pram was soon nearly full of twigs, sticks and little soft logs. The last of the afternoon light came in among the trees, at least at the edge, and I enjoyed the look of the copse itself. While Hilda and Joan worked away at packing the last few bits of wood into the pram and collecting, from a solitary bush, hazel-nuts which were too high for me to reach, I found myself staring at a distant row of trees on the further flank of the hill which showed the October colours in subtle balance – a dull-red tree, a brown tree, two foxy-red beeches, a dark sombre holly, a pale elm masked with green blossoming ivy, and, near the skyline, a clear, beautiful, buttery-yellow little tree which I knew to be a maple. In the valley the yellowish-grey willows looked fragile. We were all pink with exertion and laughter as we pushed and jolted the pram back on to the track, and decided to fill up the few remaining gaps with fir cones from the dreaded Schwartz forest.

We made forays into the dark needly wood, which smelt of resin and was carpeted with cones at various stages of development from hard and green to dry and open and to those flaking down to a core. We dashed in, filled our pockets and dashed out again. I found a spent orange cartridge which I pocketed, and some curved fir bark which I thought would also make good kindling for the fire. As we filled up the spaces in the pram, the sun went below the hill, touching the rows of trees with a momentary halo of red, and the edge of the 'forest' seemed more and more menacing; I almost saw twisted blotchy-faced gamekeepers and heard the baying of huge dogs. Hilda, though so much older, was just as easily frightened and soon hurried us away. When we turned for home both Joan and I had a hand on Hilda's as she pushed the pram in the gathering dusk back to Cobb's Corner. How we looked forward to bread and jam and tea, our fingers chilled where they stuck out from the mittens, and how pleased we were to be back in the familiar surroundings of Cobb's Corner and Crabbe's Hill. Our hushed voices rose again as we sang a premature Christmas carol on the way past Haverton's; we heard lowing from the milking shed and smelt the fresh cowpats, and faintly the distant warm milk.

We were all taken to church on Armistice Sunday, as it

was such a special occasion, even though Bill was not yet three. Now that the war had been over for a year the memorial was completed and fastened to the wall inside the church. I remember the names being intoned aloud by the curate. When there were several with the same surname I assumed that they must all have been blown up in the same ship or brought down in the same aeroplane, as the idea that brothers might be separated, even in war, never entered my head. Although the ceremony was solemn and sad, especially as it was spoken so slowly, death was not yet real to me, and it all felt very remote from me and from my world.

PART TWO

Disasters and Recoveries

CHAPTER FIVE

PRIMROSES AND PROBLEMS

I remember clearly this early period in the cottage when we seemed to be steadily prosperous and everything was All Right. My mother bought new dresses, my father kept wine in the house, we had Joe in the barn or out in the Medder, there was chicken for Sunday dinner and plenty of eggs for breakfast. My mother was always busy and always happy during this halcyon period. We were associating on equal terms, I thought, with the local gentry, and my parents were often out in the evenings. Florence had an evening dress of peacock blue and black, and kissed us goodnight smelling of something remote and wonderful, while my father down below could be heard clanking the metal as he harnessed Joe and off they went clip-clop in the trap towards the dipping light of the westering sun. The Nevilles next door would always keep an ear for us if Hilda wasn't available. The three of us didn't in the least mind being left; once we went downstairs to forage for blancmange, so delicately balanced on plate and spoon as we went up the stairs in the fading light; we invented activities involving a certain amount of getting out of bed, though Joan was insistent on a sort of Play the Game ethic and wouldn't let it go on too long. There were glossy magazines in the house. *Nash's Magazine* was a great favourite: its amazing illustrations, glossy expensive paper and ink smelling of luxury gave us a sense of privilege as we eased the stiff spine to creak open its close-bound pages. Instead of home-made cigarettes there were pricey Three Castles in beautiful black-and-green packets.

Joan shopped in the village with a pound note instead of the exact money and might be told to buy us all sweets, which made the toiling walk through the sunshine and shade of Crabbe's Hill all the more worth while. Sometimes we had Bill on foot or in a pushchair, but generally Joan and I were alone. In this period we had new macintoshes and 'bought' jerseys and grey shirts and Joan had a green kilt and rather swagger ribbons in red and gold for her pigtails, and we had tomato sauce with cold chicken or beef, and haddock for breakfast, which we ate with proper fish knives and forks which Arthur bought at the Army and Navy Stores and proudly brought home as a mark of our improved social status. One weekend he arrived laden down with parcels – a big drawing book for me, special bricks of various shapes and sizes for Bill, dolls' clothes and a needlework set for Joan, even peaches nestling in wood shavings, in a little wooden box.

This was the time when Tim Hunney was working for us in his spare time, gardening and tending the livestock. Sometimes he groomed old Joe, very gently and slowly, with curry combs and brushes, in the dark barn, which smelled of cow-cake and old straw. I sat on a tree trunk that had always been there and was used for chopping wood, while he told me about his eldest brother Henry in the Navy, and what had happened to him during the war, in a battleship. Tim played cricket for the Owslebury team; he was pale-haired, tanned, handsome, offhand, unfailingly cheerful, and whistled marvellously. In spite of their large family his father and mother were still young-looking and energetic and their small farm was very successful.

Tim Hunney soon got our wedge-shaped garden into order, and cut neatly away at the mixed hedge with a slasher. This inspired Bill to cut the small hawthorn hedge which divided the Medder from part of the garden with a pair of scissors, and though he was gently teased he persisted for a long time. I was always with Tim, sometimes 'helping', sometimes frankly hanging about; he didn't seem to mind. He would never lunch with us but always somewhere in the garden, with huge crusty sandwiches and a black bottle of cold tea; but in the middle of the morning he would accept from my mother a large mug of steaming hot tea and a hunk of bread and apricot jam passed through the scullery window. I remember her with a bright pinafore, floury arms and pastried hands, the old scales out on the stone table. The apricot jam was a speciality; she would make a winter jam out of dried apricots, and when they were piled in a basket they were, I found, leathery and tough and disappointing to eat raw, but when you spooned the jam out of the jar you always got a lumpy half-apricot which wouldn't spread, and you would smooth the runny orange fluid over the rest of the bread and save the soft substantial mouthful of apricot till last. Happiness descended as we sat on the log in the black barn, the wan spring sun slicing through the cracks in the walls and lying in a rhomboid at the open door. One heavenly morning we limewashed the little lavatory after Tim had bravely dealt with the enormous spiders and their grisly webs.

The memories flood in on me as I think of Tim Hunney. The most vivid morning must have been in late spring; he had dug over the grassy bank alongside the garden, having the sensible idea of a countryman that only land unfit for vegetables should be wasted on flowers, and suggested to my mother that he should get some primrose plants for it. I was up early that morning and had chased a Brimstone butterfly right across the Medder and had got my socks and legs soaking wet with the dew, when Tim arrived pushing his bicycle up the brick path, with a bit of canvas tied on the carrier, full to overflowing with primrose plants. I bolted my breakfast and rushed out in time to help him plant them. He had lifted them from Boydon's Wood where there were hundreds; as it was so late in the season they had floppy leaves and long-stalked flowers, some of them wilting. The earth was sweet and damp; plovers and rooks wheeled in the sky. I picked a bunch of the pale flowers for my mother, distinguishing with delight the yellow-scalloped centre from the creamy petals, and the two kinds of middle, one like a pinhead and the other like a tiny cluster of seeds, getting my fingers right down to the root to pick out the greeny-pink hairy stems. I surrounded the flowers with the embossed curving leaves, tied the bunch with a bit of raffia Tom had produced from his corduroys and took them into the cool dark scullery. My mother kissed me, untied them tenderly, put them in a little chipped jug of dull blue and stood them on the window sill in a patch of brilliant sunlight before she went back to the rhubarb pie she was making. I went back to the damp bank and the pile of primrose plants and Tim, on his knees with the trowel, whistling.

While he was clearing up and putting a high polish on the trowel, we started talking about birds. He seemed surprised that I'd never seen 'a lesser whitethroat's' – that is, a nest.

'I know one only half a mile from here,' he said, 'and I'll show you if you like.' He picked up his coat from the bush it lay on and wandered to the scullery window.

'I'm taking Pete down the road for a minute,' he said. 'What time's dinner?' He was always casual and offhand with my parents, and they seemed to like it. Down the little hill we went, with me balanced precariously on Tim's cross-bar, his knees going up and down on either side, his strong arms holding me, down through the April sunshine past Frankie Southgate's silent cottage. We swung at a perilous angle into the little lane with the gaunt beech saplings, and along the rutty mossy path where dog's mercury and cuckoo pint were glossy green on the verge, and the light came slanting through the trees. Insects like minute bits of fluff flew into the belts of sunlight and vanished again in the shade. There, in a thicket, indistinguishable to me from any other bit of the lane, we both crawled over beech mast and rotting leaves and dog violets till he pulled back a great arc of bramble and wild rose, and turned to watch my face. The nest was tiny and fragile, grass and roots, and in it were three minute white eggs with dark chaotic splodges and patches, especially at the broad end. It was secret, and it was wonderful.

As I sat eating the rhubarb pie, facing my pot of primroses up on the ledge, thinking of the lesser whitethroat, talking to Bill and Joan back from their walk with the pushchair, hearing Tim's whistle in the garden, I was full at once of excitement and peace.

It can't have been very long after this that the blow fell – at any rate it was before the summer was out. What the blow was exactly I never gathered; I only felt its results. The first hint was when I came down from bed for a glass of water and surprised them in the middle of making calculations and writing down rows of figures.

'But my dear Florence,' my father said, 'it's simply a question of getting through the next month. The commission is bound to come, and if my latest sketches aren't winners, I'm a Dutchman. Look, it's all there in black and white – £24 by the end of October . . . Shush! One of the children is coming down.'

And I came blinking into the dazzle of the room, lifting a bit noisily the latch of the door at the bottom of the stairs, and there was my father reading the newspaper, oh so casually, and he called me Old Man.

'Please can I have a drink of water?' And when I went again up the dark stairs, with my fingers round the coolness of the glass, into the creaking bedroom with the moonlight shining through the curtains, I felt an oppression weighing me down, constricting my throat.

One morning I found my mother crying over a letter; next weekend my father was unnaturally stern and even more than usually kind; the chickens, or most of them, were cooped up and taken away to beyond Baybridge, and a great bin of chicken food with them; Joe was sold, we were told to a farmer, but I suspect now to a knacker's yard. Hilda stopped coming, though once in a while she would still take us for a walk. Now the scrubbing, when it was done at all, was done by my mother. Joan became terribly brave and stiff-lipped.

'Don't forget,' she said, 'they're having a very anxious time just now and don't make a little pest of yourself.' I had mad little sessions of saving ha'pennies and speckly apples, even trying once to sell them to astonished villagers – but mainly I felt rather helpless and hopeless, unable to do anything, anxious that my father should stick up for his rights ('The man's an absolute shyster, my dear Florence,' he said again, showing her a letter) and yet not wanting him to have to plead – wanting in an unfocused helpless way simply that things should be better. The berries were out on the hawthorn bushes. It was windy and rainy at night. From somewhere my father got a shoemaker's last and repaired our boots himself, making, I thought, an impressively good job of it, with thick black stain to fill up the cracks in the heel-piece and ink over any small irregularities. There was gristly meat in the sandwiches I took to school for lunch, and apples instead of bacon after the porridge for breakfast. Tim of course was dismissed. Before the end of the autumn he was dead in an isolation hospital at Eastleigh from lockjaw: 'A bad cut on the loose part of the hand between thumb and forefinger, and then handling fresh manure, well, it's asking for it, isn't it?'

The good days had gone with that spring and summer. The nights were drawing in, and every attempt to pretend to be normal was somehow horribly poignant to me. My mother patched our clothing and darned our jerseys. At tea-time when there was only bread and marge my father would make magic passes under the plate while you wished, for paste or cheese, and magically it would taste like your wishes, or nearly. Joan was usually stoical about other people's wounds as well as her own, and hardly cried at all when she once almost sliced the top of her finger off on an old tin, but she nearly had hysterics when I grazed the fatal part of my hand on a tree root. She rushed me home, her face scarlet, trying to hold back her tears and bellowing at Bill when he couldn't keep up with us.

My mother served behind the bar at the Shearers Arms for a short period, 'just to help them out', packed us to bed before she left, and we would get out of bed and watch her cross the road and go into the Public. She was laughing and cheerful with Mr Chenery, but a bit rueful about it all the same. The good days had gone – and in a sense they have never returned. Nothing could ever again be so thoughtlessly and naturally perfect. The Old Man who sat in the garden lavatory on autumn nights was in my dreams, the limewash flaked off. Dust and fluff gathered in corners, the posh magazines got dog-eared and cut up for scrapbooks and were not replaced. At that time I was convinced that, although the primroses, Tim's primroses, would reappear soon, it could never be the same again.

Frankie Southgate was a steadying influence during our years in Owslebury. He was intensely loyal as well as very shy, and he was one of the local people we prided ourselves on knowing well; in his own way I am sure he liked us, though he never expected to be a family friend in the ordinary sense. He played the role of a stand-by, a resource, a sort of substitute father or husband, if only in the sense that it was Frankie who mended the barn door during the week, found some zinc nails to fasten down a bit of corrugated iron that had blown loose, put down poison after Florence had been frightened by an aggressive rat near the cesspit, and later doctored a sick goat.

What Arthur did in the city – at Messrs Groomes of Fleet Street – was still shadowy to me, but a good deal clearer was the art work which he now did at home, most of the time during the holidays and weekends. In the evenings Florence would be either knitting – she was an inveterate knitter – or reading aloud, while Arthur spent hours and hours bent over his work-table. He seemed to us to work implacably and inexhaustibly, often until eleven or so at night, pacing himself only with frequent cups of tea and innumerable relightings of damp little home-rolled fags. He was designing and making showcards, two-or-three-word advertisements, to be displayed on shop counters or in shop windows: *Veno's for Coughs, Drink Mazawattee Tea, Packers' Chocolate is Best.* If the design was approved by the manufacture or his advertising agency, some thousands would be printed, cut out by machine and strutted for the shopkeeper to display. The finished showcard always featured the trade name in either capitals or cursive letters. The top half of each letter might be cut out and therefore free-standing, while the bottom half was painted on the cardboard which made up the stand.

Some of the cards made the letters look three-dimensional, with a beautifully managed solid-looking edge in grey or brown or black, or delicately shaded according to where the light seemed to fall on them – *Hall's Distemper, Venus Pencils.* I specially loved these letters and spent hours doing my own, but I always had difficulty in getting the exact amount of underside to give the three-dimensional illusion: Es and Is were fairly simple, but letters with curves foxed me. So I could only admire my father's patience and skill, and try unsuccessfully to copy him.

Though I had no glimpse of this at the time, advertising in general, and perhaps this kind of advertising in particular, reflects the state of the economy pretty sharply. These funny little cards which were to become his life's work were the first to suffer from trade recessions. It may be that the switchback economy of the Hampshire cottage – from rags to riches and back again, it seemed, every few months or so – was a miniature version of what was happening in the money markets of that desperate period for Western Europe. But Arthur always believed that his work had such inherent merit that it could not fail: 'If you throw enough mud, my dear Florence, some of it is bound to stick.' So for all my childhood weekends there was a large drawing board in the sitting-room, a series of small poster-colour pots, a set of razor-sharp little knives and a range of pencils of various degrees of blackness, which we were forbidden to borrow as they were dedicated to the sacred cause of 'Daddy's Work'. On the board, or nearby, were sheets of brown strawy card, rolls of cartridge paper, sticky labels, paste pots and little tins full of pins, clips and drawing pins; one held loose tobacco and orange packets of cigarette papers, and two or three others, damp-looking fag-ends, as those home-made things went out the moment you stopped smoking them. All this equipment was locked away during the week and brought out every weekend. We shared his delight at the news that one of his showcards (they were called 'sketches') had been 'ordered', at thirty shillings or so, and during the week placed high hopes on the half-made ones – *Lipton's for Quality* in black and orange with only the L cut to shape, *Stephen's Inks* in blue and white with the apostrophe skied and outlined – till the next weekend when they would be finished, packed and sent off. There was real anguish in the cottage once when a long-awaited cheque arrived marked to 'Account Payee' – and as no one had a bank account it had to go back and be rewritten while Florence, with acute embarrassment, got essential things like tobacco and marge on tick from Cobb's village shop.

Much of our later time in the cottage seemed to include this element; our whole childhood seems in retrospect to have been a series of switchbacks – from a grinding and frequent poverty, with the subtle but permeating atmosphere of ill-concealed anxiety that goes with it, to a luxury stranger and more unlikely by contrast with the previous mode of life. Once half a ton of coal arrived suddenly and mysteriously when we were at our poorest. Two men humped the ten sacks into the barn, but were apparently under strict orders not to say where it came from.

'It's all paid for, guv,' they said to my father, and declined in spite of various pressures and even cups of tea to say who sent it.

'Sorry, guv – office told us particular not to say.' Could it be the Richardsons? We had a warm winter, but never found out who to thank.

Sometimes we ran downhill by imperceptible stages, sometimes we woke from daydreams of sherry and servants to the reality of bills we couldn't pay and broken objects we couldn't afford to replace. Yet it would be quite wrong to suggest that the motifs of Decline and Fall dominated: the merciful resilience of children is such that the negatives were not much more than a shadow on the excitements and fulfilments of our life. We had our own absorbing interests – family, school, friends – and perhaps especially for me, an increasing fascination with the rich and often hidden wildlife of the couple of square miles around the cottage: trees, plants, insects, birds; especially the last two.

Each day was punctuated with feeding the animals, when we had any, emptying the loo bucket into the cesspit as soon as it was half full and before it got too heavy for me to lift; it was my father who suggested that I should do this as the oldest male. He did the job at weekends and thought it highly unsuitable for the delicate susceptibilities of the female sex, though all the same Florence or our neighbour Mr Neville did it sometimes in the winter when it was too dark by the time I got home from school. One daily task of mine was to get the milk from the Pooleys in a dark-blue-and-white enamel can with a wire handle and a cup top. At first Joan came, and we would chatter away about the children at school or birthdays or perhaps preparations for Daddy's arrival. As I grew older I went alone, and my walk – about half a mile there and back – became a ritual opening to the day as well as contributing to my growing sense of the seasons: each day in spring a little softer and brighter, with the early leaves of the elder and the first daisies starring the verges; each day in autumn a trifle darker until frosts glazed the roadside puddles with white ice and there were angry red skies. The cows from Pooleys and Havertons passed twice a day along the stretch of road, and during the heat of summer it was dusty and cowpatted, all except the latest splashy disks dry and chaffy at the edges but still soggy enough in the centre to encourage the large dung-coloured sluggish horseflies which stung you badly on the legs if given half a chance. After a heavy summer rainstorm the narrow little road was almost impassable; no wonder we mostly wore heavy, clumsy boots. Sometimes the road became a mire of cowdroppings and straw and flies and deep straw-yellow puddles, edged with the little pineapple weed and merging vaguely into nettles and grasses.

Every day, it seemed, as I walked up the road, summer and winter, a thrush sang from the very top of the ash tree a little way from the cottage, silhouetted against the bland fluffy clouds of spring or the orange-pink winter skies smudged over with patches the colour of school ink. Like the three thorn trees, its song became symbolic for me, though of something so vague that I can't define it. Much as I liked the clumpy walk, the really fulfilling moment was when I pushed the latch of the cottage door and felt my cold face and fingers suddenly hot as my mother knelt by the lively flames of the twiggery blazing on the hearth, and served stiff porridge from the iron saucepan on the trivet over the fire where it had sat all night. On our beige cliffs of porridge we spooned brown sugar and poured over it the slightly bubbly milk from the spout of the can – my can.

Once in a while, though rarely when our economic state was sound, Florence and Arthur quarrelled, being led remorselessly into a row which neither of them chose. It started quietly enough:

'Florence, you don't really mean that.'

'Why do you think I said it, then? I *do* mean that.'

'Look, I do my level best, I work my fingers to the bone, and all you can do is treat me with utter contumely.'

'I'm not treating you with anything – I'm saying we just can't go on like this!'

'What alternative do you envisage? If they won't take my sketches, they won't! Any individual can get into this situation.' Tempo and pitch were growing now.

'I don't understand you! It's lunacy to suggest – '

'Don't call me a lunatic!'

'I'm not calling you a lunatic – though I do sometimes wonder – '

'Now you're just being nasty!'

'Don't shout at me!'

'I see no earthly reason why – '

'You and your reasons! If you'd just listen to reason . . .' They were both on their feet now, shouting. From Florence:

'Joan! Take the children into the sitting-room.' Joan

herded us like a clucking mother-hen, out of the scullery, her face flushed too, very nearly in tears. I found this infectious, and very soon the three of us were snivelling and Joan was half trying to comfort us and half listening to the shouting and noises of banged table and stamped feet next door. My heart went faster: I felt sadness and a bit of panic, but combined distressingly with all this was a small but perceptible excitement hidden in me. Holding back my tears, I went out of the front door, ostensibly to go to the lavatory, and saw through the little scullery window my parents in profile, their noses six inches apart, their mouths open, their hands flat on Arthur's ludicrous scullery table. His face was bright pink, and fury made his neck scar dark and angry-looking. He threw a roll of drawing paper on the floor but it didn't sound very melodramatic – a roll of paper doesn't produce a very satisfying noise, even when hurled down in a temper.

'Goodness knows why I married you! I can't go on like this!'

'You can always be guaranteed to . . .'

'I'm going out!' This from Florence: someone's departure on a longish walk outside the house meant at least that the row was over for the moment. Florence's angry feet stumped up into the bedroom to get her hat and coat and out she went through the back door, just missing me as I nipped back through the front door. She strode down the front path and turned in the direction of Jackman's Hill. Arthur, flushed and sorry for himself, came into the sitting-room where we were pretending to get on with our usual activities but in fact were cowering. He was elaborately gentle with us and concerned with our well-being, presenting the appearance of a loving and thoughtful man much put upon by a termagant wife. A few minutes passed in this rather strained and unnatural atmosphere, and soon I felt an impulse to run out into the dusk and find Florence. But this was mercifully not needed: the front door opened and there she was – in cloche hat, pink under her powder, half angry still but slightly inclined to relax. She said ruefully to all of us, 'I went out with no matches and no cigarettes,' and went to the table to find some. When she lit up she couldn't hold back a small giggle, and we found we could join in. We went to bed softly sweet with one another, and swimming in newly established amity.

CHAPTER SIX

MY MUSEUM

One winter evening when we were trudging back from school, Joan and I had seen a barn-owl. It was swooping and hawking along the ditch which was edged by willows heavily skirted with ivy. My mind was full of birds, or rather birds' eggs, and I spent bits of most evenings staring at a bird book, but the owl, alarmingly large and silent except for a faint swish, seemed very remote from the easy matey familiarity of eggs. He was darkish on the top and ghostly white on the underside, and I associated his swift silence with the autumn and winter mists hovering along the ditch. Last year I had found a furry brown object the size of a hen's egg, which Mr Last, the schoolmaster, told me was an owl pellet. When I picked it apart I found elaborately structured bones, bits of skin and matted fur. Now as I stared at the bird I imagined myself sized down to a shrew, cringing and unable to escape, clawed by this monster into the dizzying air and back to the nest, to contribute my bones and skin to the next ignominious vomiting of the owl.

There seemed no doubt that the owl lived in one particular pollard willow – three from the end, fatter at the base and rottener at the core than most of the others. After Christmas, with the lengthening though bleak days, I began to feel that the nesting season was upon us, and attached special importance to the early nesters and layers, partly because of the built-in attractiveness of their being out of season, like midwinter flowers or dazed, hibernated tortoiseshell butterflies waking on a warm day in January. I hadn't realised, though

I suppose it is true, that birds depending on leaf cover tend to wait till April; it was birds which nested in tree holes, like tits, or those like herons or rooks with nests too bulky or high to be concealed or reached, which began to build earlier. I studied the plates of owl's eggs – all shiny white, all more round rather than pointed, and varying only rather minutely in size. Could I, I wondered, get a barn-owl's egg? They laid up to four eggs, I knew, and I gave the pair of birds I assumed were nesting in the pollard until the third week in February to complete their clutch. Then, accompanied by Joan on a bleak afternoon, I gingerly approached the tree, intending to scramble up through the thick growth of ivy with Joan at the bottom to give me moral if not physical support. I went up slowly and with trepidation, calling down to her at intervals, 'Catch me if I fall!' and, 'Wren's nest building, hardly started' and rather faintly, 'I'm nearly at the top.' I gripped the last ivy handhold to the large rotted crown of the tree, my arms at full stretch, and then, swallowing, offering up a short prayer and yanking myself level with my elbows to the nest site, I saw with horrow and shock – an owl! A vast white owl, sitting bolt upright, a huge orange eye fixed on me, the other to my astonishment winking. Its feathers were smoothed and colour-graded, its vast claws imagined if not seen, an inch away from my chin – about to turn me into a vole. It looked so dignified and powerful, and seemed to resent having been awakened. Certainly no little scrub like me would dare to think of robbing its nest! I slithered backwards about ten or twelve feet, the ivy leaves smooth, even if the willow was rough and furrowed, and into Joan's waiting arms. Her face was red, her wide mouth terrified as she prevented me from bouncing. Some hopes for owls' eggs, but at least I was alive. A few weeks later I swapped one of my duplicates for a barn-owl's egg, but it was always a bit unpleasing because I thought it might have been a tawny or long-eared owl's, as they were all so similar; and my swapped egg had no real pedigree. I don't think I claimed that I had found it myself, but I did remember the alarming descent down the pollard willow every time I looked at it.

Jake Wharmby, who worked on the Havertons' farm, also ran a smallholding at the far edge of the village, beyond the Ship Inn. We didn't really know him but he did sometimes play for the cricket team. A distant relative unexpectedly left him a Southampton town house, and presumably some money, so he uprooted his family and moved out of the village. He had been able to sell his pure-bred Rhode Island Reds – I thought they were orange-brown really and tried to imagine what they would look like really red – his pigs and even his bees, but no one would buy his goats.

Arthur offered to give them a home in the Medder, thinking they lived on grass and would provide free milk for the family, and of course Florence would learn to milk them. Six goats arrived, most of them very young, but one was indeed in milk and another soon produced a kid and also came into milk. We discovered that goats don't in fact live on grass, being browsing not grazing animals, and we had to supplement their diet with expensive cake concentrate. The senior member of the flock impressed me by having so huge an udder that she had to straddle when she walked. The close-set, soft-looking amber eyes suggested a gentler temperament than she turned out to have. After her kid was born she became a kicker, and it was unwise to approach her except when she was feeding. None of us was sure that we liked the flavour of goats' milk even in tea, though it was all right for rice puddings and tapioca.

The goats were tethered in the Medder during the day, but at night, except in high summer, they occupied about a third of the barn. We had great difficulty in keeping them out of our two-thirds, though Arthur built up a complicated barrier of old bedsteads, old doors and miscellaneous whiskery string, binder twine and rusty ex-WD wire – perhaps from Hazeley Down, as Arthur had bought a vast roll for practically nothing.

I can remember, when the Medder was full of buttercups, having one of the nannies milked directly into my mouth – the milk warm and slightly sickly, the experience exciting and mildly improper. The tiny black-and-white kid, all legs, had a curious crablike jump, turning half-way round in mid-air and landing in the opposite direction from take-off. When I was writing to my maternal grandparents, I added a footnote: 'The little goat is dancing as I write,' which was prompted, indeed dictated, by my father when I couldn't think of anything to write, but was always thereafter quoted as my first incursion into the realms of creative literature.

How my enthusiasm for butterflies began, I am not sure. Many of the village boys collected, but in a casual and offhand way, whereas I seemed to be involved from the outset in technicalities, probably stimulated by Mr Last's advice and his rather good collection, which I was once allowed to examine in detail. To me his serried ranks of specimens were a revelation, and my fascination and envy made me decide to start a collection for myself. Teachers and adults spoke of 'Nature', but this meant little to me. I liked the design and markings on butterfly wings for their own sakes, and above all I wanted to have them for my own. The subtle differences were very important from the beginning, but no less important, were the names, which were so beautiful and evocative. The Chalk Hill Blue! The downs to the east of the cottage were exactly that, chalk hills – and therefore must surely be swarming with that opalescent inch of misty blue (though in sad fact they were unknown in the area). The Pale Clouded Yellow – the name seemed to me exactly to evoke the light gold of some kinds of honey and so ought to be common near the rows of beehives put out every April in the apple orchard behind Marwell Court. It took a while to discover that butterflies and their names are seldom related in this way.

My first nets were discarded bits of shirt fastened to a wire frame, with the ends hammered into a cane. I soon found that the material was not transparent enough – you had to be able to see the captive to kill it without injuring its wings – so Florence made me a long net of butter-muslin and sewed it on to a split bamboo frame which we curved around into the hollow end of a bamboo handle. My father later bound this with wire to make a stronger joint. I read about a killing bottle with crushed laurel leaves at the bottom, so Florence found me a jam jar with a screw top. I picked laurel leaves from the Chenery's hedge, found them quite hard to crush with my fingers or even my boots, and in the end took to chewing them into a mash. I put about an inch of this green spinach into the jam-jar bottom, pushed it down flat, and later that morning put a caught butterfly in, screwing down the top. It was admirably stupefied but to my disappointment once the jar was opened a rather good female Grayling, intoxicated by real air, flew straight out of the jar and vanished. So I tried again; this time I left a Speckled Wood for twice as long, and then rather tremulously unscrewed the lid. It stayed where it was on the crushed leaves! Success at last. I prepared a setting board for my Speckled Wood and when I turned back to the jar the butterfly which had crawled up the glass, crawled also on to my finger, clinging with its small feet. This resurrection saddened but also moved me oddly, and I felt obliged to let it go.

A bit later I was given a killing bottle bought in London and designed to kill insects quickly: it had a screw top and a plaster-of-Paris layer at the bottom of the jar, containing, presumably, the deadly cyanide. I was warned to be extremely careful with this, but when I put my nose in even for a long sniff it didn't seem to smell of anything much, though it did kill the butterflies quickly and efficiently.

Before I got hooked on butterflies and birds' eggs I had been accumulating odd little collections of various sorts – unconsidered trifles that, as it happened, interested neither Bill nor Joan. They were housed in various containers, all of which were packed together in a big wooden box which hadn't got a proper lid and was often carried out into the barn when we had visitors, as it took up a lot of room and didn't look very decorative. I had a somewhat desultory collection of coins in a tin tobacco box, including tokens of incredible weight and thickness, Chinese cash with square holes in the middles, wafer-thin Belgian centimes of zinc, then unconvincingly light and un-coin like, one or two pseudo-Roman coins with illegible inscriptions and obliterated faces, and a few paper notes of impressively large face value from countries already in the grip of post-war inflation. The paper notes were unsatisfactorily different in shape, size and thickness, and were kept together by a rubber band which was so tight that it bent the big ones half-way across, and yet loose enough to let the little ones slip through. Uncle Frank had given me some shells, including a few cowrie shells and one or two elaborate ones with flesh-pink innards and complex grey spines, difficult to pack even in newspaper. I had half-heartedly tried to get information about coins and shells but was put off by the difficulty of finding out anything about them and by the realisation that there were no rare coins in Owslebury and no shells except snail shells nearer than Southampton.

There were also separate objects: a single lion's claw, complete with surrounding fur, mounted on a little wooden shield, and a bit of metal which looked like a scrap of corrugated iron, but labelled 'Part of the Zeppelin which came down at Potter's Bar, 1918'. Potter's Bar may be a fascinating place, but to me it was, and is, only the Place Where the Zeppelin Came Down. Miss Gorman had once suggested that I should make a display of one-inch cross-sections of different kinds of wood. Several people, including Arthur and Frankie, had helped me to find samples, and I started to mount them. The only cardboard I could find was hairy and brown, and on this I fastened the discs of wood with crossed string and labelled them: 'Cherry', 'Ash', 'Elm', 'Hazel', and so forth. I found the slight variety and contrast of texture and bark quietly pleasing, but two things depressed me about it. There was nothing you could do with it except show it to people – it was the kind of mildly informative thing you might find in a real museum; disappointingly, ink takes very badly on that porous cardboard, as I had discovered too late. The names were blotted and nearly illegible, but I couldn't bring myself to remount them. I couldn't look over this collection on my own, let alone show it to people, without difficulty and a lot of unpacking. My father thought the whole undertaking 'very educational' and somehow 'good for Peter', but in the cramped cottage it was all the same a damn nuisance.

When butterflies and birds' eggs began to take over my life the whole thing showed increasing signs of getting out of control, especially as I insisted that these couldn't be housed even temporarily in the barn for fear of damage by the goats or chickens or other predators. So one weekend my father had the exciting idea that we could adapt a space exclusively for me to house my collections – in fact, a museum. Behind the sitting-room on the north side of the cottage there was a small, narrow, disused pantry, little more than the space subtended by the overhang of the thatch at the back and its heavy supporting timbers. The daylight from its window was filtered through the complex interlacings and leafy umbrella of the apple trees that leant against it. It was always cool and dark, even in midsummer. As far as I remember it hadn't been used much except as a place to put a sack of potatoes or to hide birthday presents.

Before we could organise it, the little room needed a thorough clean-out. All the family declined such a job with shudders graded into repressed (Arthur), open but giggly (Florence), semi-hysterical (Joan) and silently determined (me). So we arranged for Mrs Neville from next door, who had an enviable indifference to spiders and other livestock, to brush it and finally scrub it out: 'Oi don' take no notice o them things, no I don'.' Then Arthur and I spent a delightful morning fastening on the inner wall a set of shelves made of timber from the large woodpile in the barn. The original wide shelf by the window was to be my work surface and the new shelves my storage area. A slightly damaged and discarded kitchen chair, which tended to splay at the legs, was repaired for me to sit on, and Florence could just stand behind it if she stood sideways when I was sitting there without knocking the boxes on the other side off their shelves. For hours and hours after this I sat and worked in what quickly became called My Museum. It took over to a large extent from the earlier joys of the Medder Stores. The little window and its leaf-filtered light occupied the space between two large upright beams, and even after Mrs Neville's meticulous clean-out its corners quickly became alarmingly spidery. It was Mr Toombs who noticed the webs, and thereafter made a special job of brushing it out for me, and while I was grateful for this thoughtfulness, not to mention his heroism, I had a sinking feeling that he might merely have dislodged some of the monsters rather than killing them, and that they would be sitting waiting for me under one of my boxes, or – even worse – along the edge of a book. I loved my museum, but I got a bit bored with the lion's claw.

'Show her the lion's claw' said my father.

'And what about the Zeppelin?' said Florence.

'Now the coins, Peter, fetch them. Look at this, George – can you believe it? Five hundred marks?' I did my duty as curator conscientiously, but all this belonged to the past: it was the butterflies and birds' eggs that I really cared about.

I wasn't really very expert on birds. The passages in my bird book which I read with real fascination were those which described the nest and eggs of each species. I soon amassed a lot of theoretical knowledge about the nests and eggs of possible local species, but somehow didn't relate this properly to my real-life recognition of a couple of dozen or so birds. I had been assured by no less an authority than Mr Last that birds couldn't count, though they could tell the difference between none and some. My ethics, though minimal, were based on this, and I wouldn't normally rob a nest with only one egg in it, so that if there was only one I would mark the spot down and return later. Mercifully I didn't have to face the problem of the sea birds that only lay one egg. I was given an old book called *The Eggs of British Birds*. Its dog-eared and often loose coloured plates showed rows of eggs, the pale and white ones distinguished from the surrounding areas of white paper by dark backing shadows. But the real objects were not only different from the plates, but different from one another. I had a continual series of crises about identification, a continual temptation to delude myself, and a nagging background feeling that the tree sparrow was really a house sparrow that happened to build a rather dome-shaped nest in a bush instead of the thatch, and the cirl bunting was probably only a yellow-hammer.

Other problems piled up, too. When I started collecting eggs I was satisfied with making a hole at each end, first with a pin but soon, as I discovered that this could crack a tiny egg like a wren's, with a needle, and then blowing very hard through the fatter end. This produced through the hole in the thin end first the colourless 'white', and then, with more effort, the yolk, sometimes as a trickle of yellow, sometimes as a unit. This was the schoolboys' way of blowing an egg: but I read about more expert techniques. I needed a tiny drill to make a single hole in the fat part of the egg, and a little blow pipe to blow air in and the contents out of this hole. I would then be able to arrange the eggs in my cabinet, the hole on the underside, leaving an immaculate and apparently unmarked egg. I never reached this level of sophistication, but daily expected to. I haven't blown an egg for a very long time, but I still remember the sensation of bulging cheeks and flushed face, with Joan and Bill sometimes helping by mimetic action, and the contrast between heavy pressure from the lips and a very gentle touch holding the fat part of the egg between finger and thumb. Then I learned to take a mouthful of cold water to blow through and clean out the inside of the shell. Occasionally the chick would be already half formed and blowing would produce a sad bloodstained gobbet. This made me feel guilty, and disappointed as well if it happened to be a rare or much desired specimen, as the whole bottom of the egg fell away with it. Sometimes the egg was addled, and a hearty blow not only broke the shell but produced a foul-smelling lump of greenish matter. This I regarded as upsetting, but no more than part of the game.

Finding an actual nest was exciting enough, and fingering its contents, and calling down 'Two – no three' to Joan was even more so. Birdsnesting and its end-product, the egg, involved the tenderest, milkiest time of the year when the hawthorns were first puffed with green. There were stitchworts and yellow archangels and dog violets everywhere on the steep banks of the narrow roads, and pushing my way through a lightly shaded coppice or hunting nests of birds which build in grass always seemed a violation of privacy.

Though I was careful not to disturb the landscape more than necessary, curiousity and greed always triumphed against concern for the parent birds and their nest. How could you find a yellow hammer's nest without trampling grass and breaking hedge-parsley stems? It took me some time to look for birds flying out of hedges rather than searching the hedge 'cold', but when I did, I could focus hard on a small stretch and sometimes find the nest, often protected by brambles or dogroses or, if lower down, by nettles. Sometimes I remembered to bring my gloves, but more often just got stung or torn.

I soon got to know the most familiar nests: linnet, greenfinch, goldfinch – all rather similar – chaffinch – masked with moss and lichens – bullfinch with a twiggy platform under the well-woven cup. The domed nests like those of the long-tailed tit, spider-webbed and lichened and bottle-shaped, presented special difficulties because they were not designed to admit even a six-year-old's hand without tearing the tiny round secret entrance. The most one could do was to get two fingers in, and I remember so clearly not only the sensation of counting the warm eggs with blind fingertips, but also the horribly difficult business of working a single egg up the steep inside of the domed nest and trying to hold it, and more often than not take it. If when my right hand was doing this and I was ten feet up a prickly tree and my bare knees were tensed against gnarled wood to keep me steady, the problems of co-ordination were considerable. I often dropped the egg and felt monstrously guilty when I took another. We got to know from the playground chatter that a wood-pigeon's nest, much despised, could be distinguished as you looked up from, say, a magpie's or crow's, because it was built in such a ramshackle way that you could see bits of sky, or even the white eggs themselves, through the interlaced twigs. If a sparrowhawk had a nest in a spinney at

Longwood it would be widely known, and bolder and bigger boys than I might make the dizzying ascent for an egg. I was told of a pair of nightingales nesting in an oak wood but I never found the nest although I did have a special longing for the tiny khaki eggs like those of a doll's-house pheasant. I was once taken on a hot June night to a hollow scrape among ferns made by a nightjar and saw the two startlingly beautiful eggs. I had no chance of getting one. Best were the nests that only I found and only I knew about.

White eggs had, for me, an odd quality of their own. Some were inconveniently large – how on earth did one store or display them? You couldn't possibly accommodate a huge swan's egg in the same box as the minute wren's and long-tailed tit's. In the end I put mine – a Mute Swan's – in a clumsy cardboard box, by itself, bedded in cotton wool; though much needed for completeness it was an aesthetic embarrassment to which I never entirely adjusted. The various stone or greenish-white colours of the wild ducks' eggs were vaguely unsatisfactory. Someone gave me a gannet's egg, the actual shell of which was a beautiful soft greeny blue but totally coated with a hard chalky covering which was dirty and stained and took thumb-marks that wouldn't scrape off. The whole experience was generally displeasing in spite of the egg's rarity. The only kingfisher I knew of lived on the far side of Fisher's Pond in a totally inaccessible place, and though I could see him on my rare visits there I could only imagine the long tunnel in the bank and the four white eggs gleaming in the stench of rotting fish bones of which the nest was said to be made and which I firmly believed, improbable though it seemed. How would tender-bodied baby chicks survive with a tench's backbones sticking into them?

A favourite white egg was my swift's. The bird's long tail streamers and long scimitar wings seemed to make it appropriate that the eggs should be long too – very long, like a tiny white Conference pear. I half-pictured a long thin baby bird which could only be accommodated in such a shape. The adult bird, moreover, had many weird features like being unable to walk or take off from the ground and its high-pitched shriek, which somehow made it saurian rather than avian, so its egg had to be strange, and I was pleased with it. My specimen came from Stephen Last, one of the headmaster's sons who was lucky in living next door to Owslebury Church. When men came to repair the bell tower, the hammering and banging caused a swift to desert its nest high up in the timbers, and Stephen was given the whole nest with its four identical eggs – one for his collection and three to swap. The egg itself was sound and I blew it successfully, though with difficulty, through one pin-hole on the fat end and another off centre at the disturbingly narrow one. In my box alongside the eggs of robin, linnet and greenfinch, all of which were oval and vividly coloured, this almond-shaped and dead-white egg looked out of place; but I accepted the strange egg, though it looked as odd as a triangular postage stamp in a page of rectangular ones.

I had another box for the bigger eggs – thrush, blackbird, starling; these were really common – and the slightly more difficult and therefore more interesting eggs of the jackdaw, the swapped barn-owl, magpie, jay, rook and crow. I thought the 'carrion crow' was a special variety and didn't gather till later that it was merely what I called a crow. I had intense feelings that next spring I should find a grasshopper-warbler's nest in the grass at the edge of a wood, and I dreamed of yellow wagtails and Dartford warblers and even of dippers, unknown further east than Dorset. I read avidly everything I could lay my hands on – my own bird book, Landsborough Thompson's *Birds of the British Isles*, which I still have, inscribed 'To dear Peter on his birthday, 1921', and books lent to me by Mr Last, but I was easily confused and over-sanguine. So merlins, great-crested grebes and even storm petrels, snowy owls and red-throated divers seemed to me possible finds in my few Hampshire acres.

PART THREE

Country and City

CHAPTER SEVEN

A GROWING RANGE

Sunday morning church had become a weekly event, at least in reasonable weather. Breakfast was the same as weekdays, except that my father was there. After the chores had been done we opened the front door to remove the smell of stale fags. This was quickly replaced by the smell of black boot polish on all our best boots. The three of us had a special wash and brush-up. We were sat on the cold stone table and anything in our ears was winkled out with the squeezed corner of a facecloth, our knees were scrubbed with a nail-brush and polished off with a soft flannel. Then Florence used a stiff brush on our hair. Joan's had to be combed, and she yelped when there were knots or tangles, until finally it lay flat and shiny on her skull. Then it was decorated with her bright Sunday bows.

I half-remember a particular Sunday morning, but it may be an amalgam of several. Arthur was in dark trousers and my mother complained that his bottom was shiny – I mean his trouser-bottom. She wore a 'costume' with a dark coat over it. She put on her hat and studied the effect in a speckly mirror propped on books; then smothered herself again with the corpse-white powder which smelt of violets. She always carried an enormous handbag, which held not only a diary, a notebook, scent, money, keys, cigarette-making equipment, powder and powder puff, but also knitting, needlework, and on this day her own little prayerbook, an heirloom from her family in its plaited and embroidered case.

'I think my jacket will conceal any shine,' said Arthur.

'But this collar is a trifle frayed, my dear Florence.'

'I know. I'm sorry, but you've got most of the decent ones in town,' Florence replied.

'Never mind,' said Arthur. 'It probably won't show when my coat is on and if it does, well, Needs Must when the Devil Drives.' I never ever knew the meaning of this expression and am not quite sure of it now.

'Can you three children stir your stumps? We are liable to be late unless we put our best foot forward.' I wondered which was my best foot.

'I'm ready,' said Joan proudly, and went on her knees to help Bill tie his bootlaces. 'Look, Bill, you've got them in the wrong holes.'

'I shouldn't bother to change them now,' said Florence. 'Tie them as they are.'

Bill complained mildly but to no effect, and soon we were almost ready. Arthur had his jacket on and a buttonhole – this morning a pink rose with a good scent. He used the mirror for a moment to study the angle of the grey trilby with its black band, and then held the front door open, a bit like a doorman.

I had tied up Bunty in the barn; he was momentarily resentful, but quickly found a patch of sun and curled up across it. The stew for lunch was left simmering in the oven, flanked by potatoes in their jackets, and off we went, picking our way through the cowpats in our shiny boots, and reaching Crabbe's Hill with relief because no cows used it. Joan had gloves and a bag too, and walked sedately in her black-and-white check coat with the velvet collar, while Bill and I dragged behind or darted ahead, tempted to make a foray up the precipitous chalky bank but strictly forbidden to do so. 'Choral Eucharist' was what we were attending, and the clanging bell made Joan anxious about getting to church on time, but we reached the square flint tower before the bell finally stopped, and hurried down the slight slope edged by old yews.

The church smelt cold and clean, with a faint undertang of incense and lilies, and we bowed to the altar as we turned into our pews. You only had to genuflect, my father explained, when the host was there – I wondered a little about who the 'host' was, but I was so adjusted to the obscurity of adult vocabulary, especially on religious matters, that I never enquired, but merely shunted this off into the large siding labelled 'mysteries'.

We were then expected to kneel for a moment and pray. My father always put one hand right across his face; Florence looked thoughtful and shut her eyes: I'm quite sure she was praying not for herself but for us. I can remember my kneecaps comfortable on the padded, slightly ridgy hassocks and the front of my legs against the cool wood: the 'shelf' holding the prayerbooks was too high for my arms when I was kneeling, and it was a trifle like being crucified. Bill got the giggles at this stage but was quietened by Florence with her gloved hand. Then as we waited and the faint reverberations of the bell died away, she and I whispered. Joan, beyond her, made faces and signs to signify excitement and disappointment about the list of hymn numbers displayed on the little cross-topped board alongside the pulpit as we hunted them up in *Hymns Ancient and Modern*.

The service was long and not, to me, very intelligible, but the procession of priests, acolytes and choristers around the church was exciting. It was led by a soulful-looking figure holding an impressively big gilded cross very close to his nose, and behind him came the priest in his green cope, a colour I liked as well as any except for the creamy white of Eastertide. He was followed by banners which dipped and wheeled in the distance as if they were animate, and a pair of men in laced surplices swinging incense thuribles – which in my parents' opinion was an indication that the whole service was attractively High, yet another thing I found incomprehensible, except that the banners were unquestionably high. Then came the choir, which to my eye represented the life of man, from boys near my own age whom I knew, looking completely unlike their playground counterparts, to young men singing tenor, and finally to heavy middle-aged cantors producing a splendid bass boom as they roared out 'For All the Saints'. I shared a hymnbook with my bending mother and joined in as loud as possible, but couldn't resist watching them out of the corner of my eye as they passed by, each with a different but astonishing facial movement caused by his determination to do justice to the prolonged Alleluia.

At some point in the proceedings a collection was taken and I proudly watched my father, representing either *Decani* or *Cantorum*, as he 'explained', walk with his opposite number slowly towards the altar – I hoped his shiny trousers and frayed collar wouldn't show – and collect velvety purses and pass them back and forth along the rows on our side, looking, I thought, very grave and noble. Then the money was taken by the pair of sidesmen keeping step along the flagged floor, who handed it to the priest who blessed it. There was a prayer I always liked called the *Sursum Corda* – 'We are not worthy, O Lord, to come to this thy table'; I felt suitably and extremely unworthy, but never for years related 'table' to the altar. During this the invisible organist would play quiet, beautiful harmonies which stirred and moved me, and Florence and Arthur left us and lined up for communion inside the rood screen. I knew what it was called, but had no idea why those carved wooden spikes and circles were considered rude. Joan was left in charge of us, but we did nothing worse than flick through the hymnbook or once or twice look round at the strange, unfamiliar faces behind us. During this procedure a single bell tolled, and this we found very impressive.

At length the queue of communicants was finished. There were more hymns and an increasing tendency to fidget, with hissed reminders from Joan to 'sit still'. During the sermon, which I followed only at intervals, my chief memory is of slabs of vivid colour across the pews and paving from the stained-glass windows, and of mere yellow rectangles from the leaded clear glass in between. I found myself relating these to the sermons: the coloured patches seemed to suit the short idyllic sermons of the little curate, and the transparent ones matched the long lucid addresses of the muscular vicar.

Then it was nearly over: the blessing, a short private prayer on the knees, a final hymn, more organ music for going out to. Florence put her prayerbook again into its plaited cover and the press-stud made a pingy little sound, and out we all came into the dazzlingly bright sunshine through the porch and past the huge oak and iron door, greeting the vicar, his grey hair blown in the wind and his cassock billowing. My father raised his hat at familiar ditchers and farm-workers looking odd and unfamiliar in best brown boots and square-topped bowlers, and chatted to friends, while Joan and I stared a bit askance at the holy-looking tombs over which we played rowdy games at lunch-time throughout the week. There were two tiny old ladies who wore hats tied under the chin like those I had seen in the drawings of Kate Greenaway. They emerged from the shadowy porch and turned towards Cobbs Corner where they lived in the last of four little houses at right angles to the road and called Yew Tree Cottages. They were maiden sisters and both had some deformity which made their toes turn inwards; sweet and gentle though I knew them to be, they reminded me of a pair of circus clowns as they addressed themselves to their walk home and I felt guilty about the irresistible snigger the sight of them promoted in me.

At length we extracted ourselves. The little groups thinned out on their way up and down the roads and lanes and into the cottages smelling of Sunday dinner, and we started the mile walk back in the sunlight. Arthur carried Bill on his shoulders for the last quarter mile, while I carried his stick.

'Goodness gracious,' said Arthur after a few yards, 'you are getting a weight for a four year old, Bill old man!'

'I can nearly see over the hedges,' said Bill. 'Is the Havertons' bull in the field?'

'No,' said Joan, 'I saw him tied up in the yard, and Tom Davy said he wasn't going to be moved for a week. Oh Mummy, I'm so hungry! I've been starving ever since 'For all the Saints'. Did you put plenty of carrots in the stew?'

'Yes, darling,' said Florence in comforting tones, putting her arm around Joan's checked shoulder for a minute. 'We're nearly home and you'll be having dinner in five minutes. I'm a bit worried, though, about the fire, and I hope to goodness Bunty hasn't got loose – he could do a lot of damage if he got into the house with all Joan's dolls out on the sofa.'

'Don't be unduly anxious,' said Arthur. 'I feel sure that all is well. If the fire dropped a spark on the rug, Mrs Neville would know instantly and the back door's open. And Bunty was securely tied as per usual and is almost certainly asleep.'

So was Bill, in spite of being skied. Joan said again, her face puckered with anguish, 'Oh, I'm so hungry!' as we walked up the front path, and Arthur put Bill down gently before opening the front door with the rusty key. The stew indeed smelled inviting; Bunty was asleep in the barn, but delighted to be awakened and full of energy.

'Joan,' said Arthur as she began laying the table very fast, 'however ravenous you may feel there is no need for undue haste.'

'Oh Arthur,' Florence interrupted, 'do leave the child alone! She's hungry, and you don't know what it feels like because you never are.'

'You are perfectly right, my dear Florence. I always eat sensibly, but I do not know what hunger is.'

'Well, I do!' said Joan, as we drew our chairs up.

'And so do I,' said Bill with the air of playing a trump card, as Florence began spooning stew into the plates. There was no conversation for the next few minutes, and only one remark.

'Try not to gollop your food, Joan,' said Arthur, not unkindly. From Florence he only got a visual signal of disapproval, and Joan ignored him entirely.

It was a rich deep happiness for us all to be together. After dinner and the washing-up Florence and Arthur snored gently in their two armchairs by the fire, while Joan and I played bossy shopkeeper and inept customer in the Medder Stores, and Bill, after joining in for a while, wandered off along the hedge on his own devices.

One spring morning, Aunt Grace and Auntie Boughty arrived from Winchester in a taxi which drew up outside the cottage. They had given the driver elaborate instructions – 'more or less opposite the Shearers Arms in Owslebury Bottom but a bit further on' – and all three looked triumphant at having found us. Florence and Joan rushed out to greet them, and the driver made rather a display of opening the taxi door. I followed more slowly, and they bent down to kiss me, all carnation perfume and soft kid gloves. Florence was both proud and rueful about the cottage, but Aunt Grace said it was lovely. The taxi driver was paid and drove up to Havertons to reverse, and I waved him off on his return journey. As the oldest male it was my job to hump their luggage into the cottage. They were to sleep at the Shearers because we hadn't enough room, and soon Mr Chenery arrived to take their bags over, but not before Aunt Grace had made a great to-do of finding the presents. There was a bottle of sherry, and some magazines for Florence, and for us three children a large flat box of sweets, each sweet nesting in a separate brown frill, and including a lot of my favourite marzipan. Florence opened the bottle and Aunt Grace accepted what she called 'a drain' – enough, it seemed to me, to wet the bottom of her glass; but Florence's full glass made her by degrees a bit pinker and more voluble. Joan, Bill and I quietly chewed sweets; (nobody noticed that I had pinched most of the marzipan, as they varied in colour and shape) until Florence said firmly that we should ruin our dinner if we had any more. My contribution to that dinner had been to dig extra potatoes for our two guests, and they were sizzling quietly around the little joint of beef in the fireside oven, now beginning to smell wonderful in spite of all those sweets.

Aunt Grace seemed to me immensely old and shaky; yet she charmingly had a faded sparkle in her eyes which I still remember with affection. Like my mother she had smothered her face with powder, but she also wore a little lipstick on her wrinkled and puckered mouth, making a pattern like iron filings round a magnetic bar. Her mouth looked sad when she was talking and seemed bracketed by her powdered jowls: like the other senior members of the family hers were pronounced, and she had rather pouchy eyes. Her hair was grey and permanently waved in the then-modish style, close to her skull, and her long crystal earrings made a minute sound when she bent down to me. She had never married, but I was always surprised to see my mother's letters addressed to Miss Jennings, since 'Miss' meant to me a girl no older than twelve or so. It was hinted in the family that she once had a sweetheart who was killed in the Boer War which she always called the South African War and which seemed to me a very long way back in history. This made her brave and sad – a telling combination in my small experience. She lived for years with Boughty, an ex-professional piano-teacher, now very arthritic and with an odd sideways shake of her head which seemed to express doubt or negation even when she was being warmly approving. Her real name, it was explained to me, was Mrs Boughton, and her husband was dead. Both wore lots of jewellery and both tinkled as they moved about.

Aunt Grace was continually thoughtful about the needs of other people. Walking up to Owslebury Top with me when my mother sent me to the village shop, she decided to buy a present for Florence, and what she said as she groped in her handbag with gloved fingers – 'I should like about a shilling's worth of cigarettes, please' – became another family saying.

She had a way of scaling herself down to us, and I thought especially to me. The interest she showed in my activities seemed absolutely genuine and unpatronising, between equals. She walked across the dewy grass of the Medder with her skirts drawn up a bit to see a nest in the hawthorn hedge and seemed to like it as much as I did. She sat beside me on half my chair in the little Museum while I took her slowly through my collections with appropriate anecdotes for most specimens. She peered at a robin's egg 'just like milky coffee – and so tiny!' and when I held up a Red Admiral by its pin and showed her the ash-and-pink underside she delighted me by calling in Auntie Boughton, who bent to get through the entrance, her head shaking even more than usual.

'Boughty, do just look at this! Isn't it incredible?' I swelled with pride, as if I had designed it myself. Aunt Grace took the Medder Shop with engaging seriousness, buying packets of dock-seed tea from us with mallow seeds. These we used for money as they were disc-shaped and filed so neatly in their containers, but were also edible. She was very patient too with Bill and helped him cut things out of coloured paper when he couldn't manage the scissors.

One evening of her stay, by a sudden impulse and without asking Florence, she took Joan and me out in the moonlight just before bed, and we gazed with delight at the cold bright moon, smiling through the tapioca clouds and the sprinkle of bright icy-looking stars. We walked half-way to Pooleys and back, and we loved it – it was so fresh and novel.

Aunt Grace's continual delight in our doings and our surroundings, our neighbours and every nuance of our country life, gave it a curious edge and made us – or me, at least – want to boast about its rusticity, beauty and uniqueness. Boughty was a sweet soft shaky echo, but it was Aunt Grace who made us see how interesting we were – and I was very sad when the taxi came and their suitcases were loaded up and we had lots of scented kisses and scented gloves and last-minute rememberings of rolled umbrellas. They pressed a florin into each of our willing hands, and I watched the little taxi climbing up Jackman's Hill. As it vanished from sight I thought sadly of their being drawn back to the mysteries of London, but remembered that in the summer holidays we should see Aunt Grace again.

Around that time I found myself steadily more involved in the world of school. The day we broke up for the Easter holidays, Miss Gorman announced the names of those who were 'going up', and I was among them. On the first day of the summer term I was one of the littlest of the biguns; but the class distinction between littluns and biguns was blurred by some presumably backward boys, who seemed enormous to me, still attending some of the littluns' lessons, in some cases finding difficulty in getting their legs under the tiny desks.

I remember only a handful of the pupils, and most of those haven't got names, but a few have. Spud Newton lived in a tiny overcrowded cottage in a lane out of the village on the way to Marwell Court; he was an enormously tall, powerful and knowing boy – red-haired and freckled. These freckles were not only all over his face, but also right across his shoulders, arms and chest, as we saw when he stripped to the waist to sunbathe in the churchyard – an odd and daring thing to do at that period. He seemed to know everything and take a superior attitude to all the activities of me and my age-group, though he was a bit more respectful to his contemporary, Joan, if only because she was much cleverer than he and could sometimes help surreptitiously with his classwork. Spud led and organised many of our playtime activities and seemed fearless and uncompromising in his attitude to authority. All the boys of my age hero-worshipped him.

Tim Hunney's sister, Sally, straw blonde, her clothes so washed that the colours had dimmed, was among the biguns, and I had the sensation of going hot when she appeared, so that I was continually following her with my eyes and yet wishing that she wasn't there. Her brothers, Jim and Gerald, were roughly my contemporaries, and looked like Tim and the rest of the family; their shirts, like Sally's frocks, were bleached and faded. The washing line at their farm was always loaded, and their clothes smelt of wind and fresh air. Also among the biguns were two of Mr Last's four sons, Stephen and Hugh; the older ones boarded at Peter Symonds School in Winchester. All four were more interested in sport that I was, but we spent many hours that summer making complex wigwams of boughs and evergreens and moss when we were deeply involved in a Red Indian game. This was played in a belt of woodland which sloped sharply down to a high-fenced waterworks with a pump, which made a regular asthmatic thumping noise night and day. Soon we had enlarged an extensive maze of rabbit holes into an underground hut deep and wide enough to hold several of us at once, sitting on facing earth seats as in a miniature railway carriage. This digging was not as difficult as it sounds, the soil under the trees being damp and soft with many years' accumulation of leaf-mould. There were steps down, which we trampled so that they were reasonably firm, and we took a lot of trouble roofing the main chamber with branches of dying wood covered with small pieces of yew or holly, bracken and moss to look as much as possible like the surrounding woodland floor. Over the steps was a kind of lid which we could replace when we were at the bottom and thus be completely hidden, a very pleasing sensation. Six of us sat in two threes, knees touching, in a dark-green shade smelling of soft leaf-mould and yew leaves, sucking and passing round a home-made pipe of peace. We greeted one another with raised hands, and romped round the woods with bows and arrows while Joan, Sally and some other girls had to sit in the cool secret hole with feathers in their hair, because they were squaws and as everyone knew they had to stay in the wigwam, perhaps occasionally chewing bark.

Arithmetic lessons at school came appropriately after religion, and I found them equally difficult, so it was nice to get them over early each day. There was a good deal of addition and division done with elaborate neatness in two columns with 'Ans =' as the stirring climax of each entry. We learned the rivers round the English coast starting with the North East and going clockwise all round the coast to Carlisle. We learned the kings of England in order, with their dates, and I can still remember them apart from a tendency to get snarled up at about the fourth Edward. In my mind each king had a colour and a persona which was quite unconnected with anything about the real man or his reign, and came solely from the rhythm; Richard I was neat, fresh and young because his dates jingled – 1189-1199; William and Mary

(1688-1702) were one flesh in every sense, reigning hand in hand; and I felt sorry for Edward VI whose reign, parroted with the others, 'April-June 1553' was so pathetically short, though a beautiful time of year. We drew and painted; I liked this and developed an early talent for copying bits of herbage which we brought on drawing days. I sketched oak-apples on a leafy twig and found the oakleaf margin easy enough but the undulations of the leaf surface impossibly difficult. We learned to write from copy books and I got the same kind of pleasure in exact copying, when I could manage it, as I had received from a pile of identical tea packets in the Medder Stores, squared up and 'in rhyme'. Nature Study was altogether different and nicer because it was nearer my own growing interests. The school had a pressed-flower collection which was shown and passed round. Many of the older specimens had lost their colour, and I couldn't work up a lot of excitement about the habitat of a two-dimensional forked growth in greenish straw with petals the colour of uncooked egg-white, whatever it claimed to be. Fresh flowers were also brought, by pupils as well as teachers, and their names written on the board, though I precociously developed a taste for the Latin names which were printed next to the English ones in an old two-volume copy of *Flowers of the Field* we had at home. While birdsnesting in a coppice I once found a Herb Paris – a lily the book said, and a likely story that was, I thought – with whorls of leaves topped with a single green flower. I took it to school and blushed with pride and embarrassment when it was identified, held up for admiration, written on the board, and earned me commendation in front of all the others.

There was a system of stars: blacks were for workday successes like three correct 'Ans =' in a row, five blacks made a red and five reds a gold. One competition which ran weekly with star rewards during the summer months was flower arrangement. Joan and I, and later Bill, worked hard at this, and took bundles of flowers collected on our walks over the weekend for the Monday morning display. I can remember the hard pincushion heads of scabious, mauve and fringed, which we though looked good with pinkish marjoram. Sometimes there were dogdaisies with their fluted white petals, and wild oats, their heads hanging elegantly but with horribly fragile stems. Yet somehow the winners were always better than ours: the grasses had longer stalks and included a haze of the beautiful quaking grass. They often had fine stems of the clear pink sainfoin and always rarer flowers like setterwort or the subtle burnet. They were always more elegant than ours, which side by side with the winners looked stubby and over-leafy on the window sill. Still, we often came fourth. By the end of the term you might have an uncountable number of gold stars opposite your name and if you came top you were given a book prize. This was always a volume of bible stories, but with coloured illustrations full of biblical figures in Arabian robes and head-dresses. Mine had a handsome coloured label stuck in the front with 'Peter Hewett, top of class I Summer Term 1921' beautifully written in copperplate.

All the same, playtime remains more vivid. We played cricket in front of stumps chalked on the playground wall, and a ragged kind of football with a tennis ball which Spud and his friends rescued daringly from the school gutter by climbing up when it occasionally landed there. We bartered fag-cards and stamps. We went to Granny Baker's shop during the lunch hour and bought Locust Beans at a penny for eight ounces; Packers' chocolate, greasy and sweet, broken into bits and powdery on the surface, for four ounces a penny; liquorice sticks or bootlaces at two a penny, and for a ha'penny, tissue-paper triangles of sherbet with hollow liquorice tubes in two corners through which you sucked up the powder and got a fizzy mouthful. For a ha'penny you could buy a little main course on a cardboard disc – a tiny chop in red and white, two bright green peas, one yellowish potato. These little objects were favourites with Joan, even though she expressed disappointment that they didn't taste like grilled chops and vegetables. The shop was very dark and low and smelt of tar and treacle, while Granny herself, tiny, thin haired, with gold-rimmed spectacles, smelt of violet cachous and damp paper and could never hear what you wanted the first time you asked. Her veiny arthritic old hands were unsteady with the little brass weights of the scales and fumbled with the paper-bags; whichever size she chose, it was often too small in the end.

At lunch-time we played lots of heavy-booted, running-about games: I still remember the sound and feel of kicking tins on the concrete playground and between the tombs in the churchyard. If you were about to be caught, booted or punched, you could deflect the attack by crossing your fingers and shouting, 'Fainites!' One favourite was a game for boys only called 'Jump Jimmy Neckers'. I had no idea what this meant or how it was spelled; could it possibly be 'Knickers'? In this game two teams of four each were picked – I can remember the anguish of being picked last – and one boy propped himself firmly with his hands against the wall and his trunk parallel to the ground: another propped himself behind with his hands on the hips in front, until there were four in a row. Then the leader of the opposing team took a run from a measured spot and leapt over as many of the backs as he could, and the horses then tried to shake him off on to the very hard asphalt surface while everyone shouted the lines:

> Jump-jimmy-necker, om bom bay
> Om bom bay, om bom bay

Break down horses, break down horses,
All over, all over.

I can't recall the scoring, but it was elaborate. I have never forgotten being a horse with some huge-booted, strange-smelling boy clinging for dear life to my back, and even worse the giddy feeling when I was on top being swung and jerked from side to side like a rider in a rodeo. Some of the girls watched and Joan was inclined to shout, 'Pete, be careful!', embarrassing me acutely in front of my friends. However, nothing more serious than bruises from kicks or falls ever seemed to result.

Every day there was Joan, strong, conscientious, anxious, utterly reliable, to jolly me along and cosset me gently. On a bright dewy morning the buttercups pollened our boots with delicate yellow as we plodded up the grassy footpath. As soon as we arrived at school and ran up the brick steps and through the open iron gates, I rejoined the male trade union of the playground and turned my back on her, but I was always pleased to be going back with her along the tussocky field-path. One long baking afternoon in July we hurried back to tea, and I dashed out afterwards on my own pursuits till bedtime, happy in the thought that the summer holidays started on Friday. 'Only a hundred and eighteen hours from now!' I remember thinking.

CHAPTER EIGHT

MORE COLLECTING

The hundred and eighteen hours soon vanished, and the first morning of the holidays found me squaring my shoulders for a serious and sustained effort to collect the many butterflies I'd seen at inconvenient or impossible times. I had watched them float over the playground, vanish over the hedgerow (was it a Dark Green Fritillary or merely a rotten old Meadow Brown?) or settle with wings outspread on a garden flower, just as I was called in to dinner for the third time.

Latin names were a further enrichment once I knew the insects and their English names, and they quickly became intimate appendages themselves. At seven and a half I knew the Latin names for a fair number of the sixty-four English butterflies – at any rate the bigger and more distinct ones – though I had my own methods of pronunciation. The names themselves seemed beautiful to me: *Vanessa atalanta*, for example, seemed exactly right for the gorgeous blacks, reds and white of the Red Admiral. Equally perfect for my favourite Orange Tip was its Latin name *Euchloe cardamines*; this looked exactly right on the label but I had difficulties with pronunciation and made it *You-klow card-a-mines* rather than *You-Cloe car-dam-in-eys*.

Although I had solved some of the problems of catching and killing these little beauties, I still found I had a long way to go before I could aspire to the peerless elegance displayed in any corner of one of Mr Last's cabinets. Butterflies, I soon realised, nearly always die with their wings folded, and if you want to display their usually more attractive upper sides, they had to be persuaded to stiffen in death with the forewings spread so that they made an angle of fifty degrees or so with the line of the body. Once they had stiffened or 'were set' it was impossible to alter their shape. This process, which used pins, setting boards, and thin strips of tracing paper, took a fortnight, and attempts to speed this up and put specimens in my collection after a week had to be abandoned when more than one drooped and flopped despondently after a day or two, and ruined the whole effect.

I had tried to make my own setting boards. My first one was three inches or so wide and about a foot long. Pins, I found, always bend when driven into wood, so I nailed two strips of cork, one on each side of the board, leaving a slot down the middle to accommodate the butterfly's body. Pins would damage the wings, so they were used to hold down strips of tracing paper to keep these in position, the pins being placed as near as possible to the wings without actually piercing them. The feelers or antennae, even more fragile, also had to be in the right position. There was no shortage of tracing paper in the cottage, though during the week when Arthur was in London it was like contraband.

I soon discovered that the channel itself had to be corked to avoid bending the vital pin which impaled the butterfly through the chest, and this involved the difficult and dangerous operation of slicing the cork in half. Even when I had a complete board to my liking I found it would only take butterflies of a certain wingspan, and the smallest ones I caught almost slipped down the crevasse and were lost to sight. So I decided I must have a series of boards of graded sizes, and badgered my father the moment he arrived for the weekend, and waited patiently through what seemed an elaborate supper and a whole week's accumulation of gossip before he could attend to me. He solved the problem neatly, glueing the cork instead of nailing it on, and using a beautiful little object he told me was called a gouging chisel to take out the slot in a long curved tongue of shaving. Fortunately during this period there was what he called 'no undue pressure' for showcards to be finished, and he found time to make me a series of boards in graded sizes, the smallest, my favourite one, an inch across for familiar garden butterflies like Small Heaths and Holly Blues and such small deer. I found the technicalities and difficult procedures were much less pleasing than the rich and simple delights of chasing and catching butterflies, and waiting a whole fortnight was frustrating indeed. But I hung on to the belief that it was all worth while for the ultimate reward I firmly foresaw – a boxful of immaculate beauties with exactly symmetrical wings and two feelers apiece.

I soon got to despise ordinary pins from the village shop, and my father got me some special plated black ones in various sizes. I had a strong feeling of frustration when I looked at my collection for the hundredth time and saw the asinine grin of a big kitchen pinhead on two of the butterflies, while the others were all neat and black. Unwisely I decided to change the pins. One of them I managed to get out, but it left a fairly big hole in the hard case of the thorax, and that butterfly insisted on sliding down to the bottom of the pin and skewing round on its loose anchor whenever I lifted the box, spoiling the uniformity-plus-variation that even then I felt was the exciting key to the beauty of the whole display. The other was a rarity, the only specimen I ever had of a variety of the beautiful and not uncommon Silver-Washed Fritillary with an odd greenish-brown look to it, called *valesina* (I called it *vaselina*, and very appropriate the name seemed to its colour): a fine rare insect ruined by its great silvery pin, since it had been caught in the days before 'I really knew what I was doing'. With infinite care I prised at the obnoxious pin, felt the stiff body moving, and finally got it out. Even the biggest of the black pins slid through the hole far too easily, so I decided to make another hole, just above the old one, which would not show anyway. The pin went through the horny case, and then met resistance. I pressed, and the whole body came apart in a second. Four *valesina* wings lay forlorn on the white paper. I cried then, and even a Large Tortoiseshell I caught the next day was no substitute for the gap in the box with the little label which stressed its emptiness.

This particular year the five-acre field which ran behind the Medder had wheat on it. It was backed by a weedy ditch, full of yellow-spired mulleins in season, and the three thorn trees had their roots on its far bank. The men with the reaper and binder arrived very early on a cloudless day in the holidays – almost at dawn, it seemed, though they had waited until the dew was off the field. One man drove the binder, the two others picked up the bound sheaves and stacked them eight at a time into beautiful stooks. Once I was allowed to sit up on the box alongside the driver who sat firmly in a buttock-shaped seat made of pierced iron; he was bare-armed, and wore bleached corduroys held up at the knees with leather straps. It was strange to be up close to my three thorn trees, as they made such a sharp and beloved image when seen from the bedroom window but lost their significance at close quarters; they were just three rather windblown hawthorns, with green berries beginning to redden. When half the field was reaped I was fascinated by the step-shaped line between cut and uncut field, with twining convolvulus and creeping speedwells visible along the edge, and by the nibbling action of the binder's clanking windmill. I took my lunch out on a plate and sat on the sheaves with the three men, watching them eating thick cheese sandwiches washed down with cider. They pushed back their caps to reveal a crescent of white skin below the hairline, and a triangle of red-brown was exposed by the collarless neck of a thick flannel shirt under the waistcoats they never seemed to take off. There was a strong smell of straw and sweat.

We hadn't noticed many rabbits in the field, but a small gang of boys, including Teddy Chenery, appeared with sticks when the last rectangle was being reaped. There seemed to be nothing in the small remaining strip, and the boys stood round in a lackadaisical and relaxed way, when suddenly someone shouted, 'There's one!' and there was a mad rush after a zigzagging white scut. Teddy did more talking than running, and I ran only half-heartedly, as I couldn't bear to be responsible for the crack of stick on bone if I had really caught up with my quarry. All the same, two boys caught rabbits, dispatched them reasonably neatly, and carried them home on the end of their sticks. All *I* got was cornhusks in my socks.

For several warm nights the stooks stood beautiful in the moonlight with a placing shadow for each. I loved their shape and tried with little success to draw them. In a few days a pair of blinkered horses pulling a tumbril was led round the field to 'pick up'. Two men pitched the sheaves neatly with their forks up into the stationary cart, and they were placed skilfully by the third standing on the top of the wagon. In the end the load looked full to toppling and yet was perfectly firm, as I found when I was helped up on to the topmost layer and had a bumpy ride across the stubble and down Gough's Lane. Then I said goodbye and slithered off the back and down to the ground by the iron stays on the tailboard.

We had permission to glean the field after the harvest. So as well as running our few remaining chickens on it – and indeed there was no way of stopping them as the field was unfenced from the Medder – we spent many hours in the heat collecting the scattered ears and grain into a paper-lined shopping basket, and separately collecting the loose straw into a box for nesting the hens. Florence came when she had time, and it was much more fun when she did because we all sang – a medley of hymns and 'community songs'. I remember our favourite *Sweet and Low* trilling out over the stubble:

> Father will come to his babe in the nest
> Silver sails all out of the west.

When Florence was busy, Bill and Joan and I did some gleaning – the idea was to gather as much as possible before the rooks and jackdaws got the lot.

Joan and I did one morning alone, and she insisted on dividing the field into measured strips with a stick at each end. I found it a bit frustrating to be forbidden to take a tempting handful of ears because they lay just outside the marked area. I was already dimly convinced that the best blackberries were always out of reach and the grass always greenest on the other side of the fence. So when, after an hour timed by her watch, she went into the house, I cheated shamelessly for a while, and then loafed about, thinking of the lapwings nesting on the bare plough last March. The field smelled mainly of straw, but there was also a residual smell of dead poppies and the dried remnants of corncockle. The latter gave me a small pang as I was specially fond of this plant and fancied it for competitions at school; it was tall, with big solitary flowers of bright magenta petals pleasingly arranged in a rayed disk with the green calyx making a star for the flat flower-head to rest on. It lived only in the middle of standing corn and didn't flower till the cereal crop was almost ripe, and then it made a lovely contrast with the bleached straw and russeted cornheads around it, but couldn't be reached without trampling the crops. I kicked the withered growth where it lay among the stubble.

Eventually Joan appeared, climbing the steep earth steps from the garden, her straw hat the same colour as most of the landscape. Then she zigzagged across the Medder with an overfull cup of cocoa in each hand, and managed an erratic balancing act over the prickly stubble. When she arrived, though her eyes were firmly fixed on the already skinned-over cocoa, I was working earnestly and in an orthodox way.

It seemed to me that the richest deposits of loose grain must be where the stooks stood, and I had a theory that if we could discover or work out the pattern in which they stood we should fill many baskets. It was a good theory but I never made it work. Small frustrations were mixed with this hot but pleasant activity. The grains lying among the stubble were very difficult to get hold of; gloves I found were useless as well as intolerably hot, and without them the stubble scratched and tore our hands. Joan insisted that the complete ears were the important thing, but I continued stubbornly to grope with my open hand among the stumps, getting at best a finger and thumb full for my pains; it was like trying to pick sand out of a thick-piled rug. Once or twice in a long morning we shared the humping of the quite weighty basket – put the wheat ears into a sack, and watched the grain fall like heavy water into the old tea-chest in the deliciously cool and shadowy barn.

The holiday I spent in London that September made a rich contrast to the life in Owslebury Bottom. As the time for departure grew near, we got more and more excited. We would all climb into one bed and talk in whispers long after we were supposed to be asleep. My maternal grandparents had now moved to an even more luxurious house, in Bayswater. We constructed in the barn a version of a London taxi out of an old tarpaulin and some wooden boxes, with an ancient iron plough seat for the driver and a window at the back, and we 'drove' it for hours through Bayswater and

Notting Hill Gate. Our idea of really posh talk was 'Do come in and have a fruit.' We used lavishly the few London place names we knew, pointing out the stiff cracked old harness hanging on the worm-eaten walls, as Lancaster Gate, the little window hammocked with spider webs as Selfridge's, and the open, crazy door of the barn ahead as Marble Arch. We got this muddled with Hyde Park Corner, since both had stone archways as centrepieces, and even now I have to think twice before I am sure which end of Park Lane is which. We also played outdoor games based on London: one took place on the tiny road outside Morestead Church which had a real metal lamp-post outside, unique in the area, and therefore easily enabling us to conjure up Bayswater Road. Bill made the car and bus noises, and Joan and I carefully looked both ways along the empty cowpatted road, before we stepped off the imagined pavement and found our way through the traffic to the other side and thus to the glittering shop windows we saw among the grey boles and swaying branches of the beech trees.

After a period of increasingly urgent preparation with Joan and Florence mending, cleaning, pressing and darning, the big day dawned. We were up unusually early, and had a bigger breakfast than usual because 'it would be a very long time before we had another proper meal'. At length everything was ready, and the luggage – a large Gladstone bag, a small trunk, Florence's huge bag-for-the-journey, Joan's handbag and the bulging satchels for Bill and me – all stood on the floor near the door, as if we were planning a midnight flit. We took Bunty over to Teddy Chenery, who was going to look after him while we were away. And then, of course, there was a long, long wait.

At length I was posted to act as sentry at the front gate. For what seemed ages I stared up the little leafy lane until at last the trap appeared, with Mr Flower the carrier bent over in the driving seat behind his fine roan mare, Betsy, clopping proudly down the road in the sunlight. I rushed indoors. We flung ourselves on the baggage, as if we were catching an aeroplane, fell over one another – 'Mummy said I was to take this one!' indignantly from Joan; a howl from Bill who had fallen against a chair and grazed his knee. And then we were outside as Mr Flower drew up, raised his high-crowned black bowler courteously to my mother, smiled slightly behind his dark walrus moustache, and let down the little round metal step so that we could get aboard. He handed my mother in, let Joan and me climb up, and finally lifted Bill in. A low seat ran along each side of the trap; the whole thing was insubstantial, and listed backwards. A coop full of nervous hens stood near some packages at one end, and our baggage was piled into the middle. Almost before we sat down Florence was screwing up a handkerchief and wetting it with Bill's spit to clean his dirty face again. We started down the little slope past the Shearers, the proud roan's neck arching jauntingly and catching the sunlight. Teddy took the big front-door key from my hand with some difficulty as he had Bunty under one arm; he shouted goodbye and tried to wave in spite of these encumbrances. A momentary sadness in my throat at the sight of the diminishing Bunty was quickly overtaken by pleasurable anticipation. Mingled with the strawy leathery smell of the trap was a strong holiday smell of the boot polish on my enormous shining boots. Joan would certainly be sick at any moment.

But there was something calming about the slow steady progress of the trap. On each steep hill we all got out and Mr Flower led the mare with the bridle, having secured the rear board again so that the luggage wouldn't slide off. He was never a loquacious man and took our frantic dialogue calmly, answering only direct questions in a slow deep voice; his Hampshire burr made him seem grave and conscientious. When progress was slow and the landscape samey, Bill tended to wander off to pick up stones or snail-shells, and I had to hold his hand to help him on. At the top we all piled in again, and once more dipped through the long tunnel of trees. At Morestead Church we picked up a brown paper parcel from an odd-looking fair-haired girl, and down the slope beyond the derelict army camp we delivered a package to a little house drowned in ivy and overhanging elms. Soon after this we came out on to the contrasting hot open downland. When at last we reached the top of the heath where the dazzling white road took a sharp turn and we saw Winchester and the glittering river below us, we were quite calm, and curious rather than excited. Then Joan *was* sick, suddenly and dramatically. Within two minutes she was smiling bravely, though her retching over the side of the trap had brought tears to her eyes. Still, it meant, probably, as she said, that she would survive the train journey itself without being sick again.

We stared at the cathedral which looked in the distance like a little toy. We could see the huddled house roofs, their ridges sharp-shadowed, the hills beyond, the outriding feelers of the New Forest in the distant haze, and felt ourselves tiny and trickily balanced on the delicate spokes of the trap wheels and the equally delicate four legs of the roan. I was rather relieved when Mr Flower pulled up again and said the weight was a bit much for Betsy and we really ought to walk the next few hundred yards. There was excitement when we saw a motorcar coming up the hill, and amusement when it stalled and spluttered and let out clouds of smoke and vapour as it struggled up. Then we came to a gentler gradient, and for the last time went through the performance of decorous handing-in (Florence), scrambling up (Joan and I), being lifted (Bill). We settled down on our facing seats while Mr Flower once more lifted the step, refixed the tailboard, replaced the metal pegs into their big rings, walked slowly round to the front, heaved himself up to the driving board, took the whip out of its socket and shook the reins. All this so that we should arrive in triumph along the wide sloping road of the town centre with the statue of King Alfred dominating it. Florence's fob watch said that we had three quarters of an hour in hand – she was always ludicrously early for any appointment. So we went into a Dainty Tea-shoppe and had bottles of very fizzy colourless lemonade, while she drank tea. Mr Flower had taken our luggage to the station and now we walked there, not without pauses to stare at toyshop windows, though Joan, unfamiliar in gloves and new red ribbons, was already getting anxious about missing the train.

Winchester and its station was a half-way stage, in terms of scale, splendour and urbanity, to the magnificence of London itself; the tiny cottage in the tiny village already seemed miles behind us in time and space. I thought of it with affection and mild superiority. We were given pennies to buy comic papers at the bookstall. We found a carriage where my mother could sit with her back to the engine and she got her knitting out of the 'bag-for-the-journey'. Then we settled down with calmness and decorum and heaven knows what interior excitement, to the long train-ride.

I remember little of it beyond a dazzled sequence of views, a great deal of fidgeting and standing in corridors, a series of unnecessary visits to the train's lavatory, and a sense of bliss as I looked through the window at an unfamiliar and beautiful landscape and then down again on to my lap at the current *Comic Cuts*, with the latest illustrated adventure of Weary Willy and Tired Tim.

At Paddington we were met by my father, who had extracted himself from his work and stood anxiously sucking a fag beyond the barrier. We groped desperately for tickets, our shoelaces came undone and we dropped our comic papers on to the platform and had them trampled on. Then we were in a taxi, surrounded by shining metal and deep black leather. We hung on to the woven straps, urged my father to use the built-in ashtray, stared again at our pile of luggage and school satchels alongside the driver, and wondered if they would fall off at the next turn. But they never did, and we drove at a fantastic and whirling speed through the back roads of Lancaster Gate, to emerge triumphantly at the wrong end of Inverness Terrace.

Number Two Inverness Terrace was a large house, part of a very late Georgian row of twenty or so. The portico was pillared: there were three storeys up, and one down at basement level for the servants. The road was very often hosed down and always wonderfully clean and shady, unlike the fairly scruffy-looking Bayswater Road at the end, with the blown newspapers wrapping themselves round the railings of Kensington Gardens. The house seemed unbelievably luxurious inside, with extremely lofty rooms. The ceilings were finished in beautiful moulded plaster with an elaborate centrepiece I often looked at, from which hung the fringed satin lampshade with its four bulbs. The electric light itself was a remarkable novelty, especially when we were allowed to turn on the standard lamp or the desk lamp. So was the upright piano with the walnut frame, so were the rows of glass-fronted bookshelves with uniform ranks of encyclopedias and sets of books. There was a magazine rack full of glossy monthlies, and a copy of *The Times* on the desk. The furniture was either leathery and cold to the backs of my knees, or plushy and yielding.

CHAPTER NINE

LEGENDARY LONDON

On the afternoon of our first complete delectable day in London my grandmother took me, although it was still summer, to a matinée at His Majesty's Theatre in the Haymarket. We were to see Maskelyne and Devant, the Internationally Celebrated Conjurors, Magicians and Illusionists, at my special request, as I had been fascinated by stage magic since my first visit in the previous year. As we came out between the pillars and down the whitened steps, I was conscious of Jenny's appearance and proud to be walking with her. She was an impressive figure, not tall but well-rounded, indeed rather wasp-waisted for that waistless period. She was wearing a long cream dress trimmed with violet. I glowed in her cheerful warmth and approval. She showed a kind of open unreserve, almost brashness, which I was not used to from adults, as though it was self-evident that everyone loved everyone else. We walked together down Inverness Terrace, and she took my hand to cross the road though I was a bit old for it, but I didn't mind, being, as I was, a country boy unfamiliar with town traffic. In contrast with the shady terrace, Bayswater Road was in bright sunshine, and she impressed me greatly by stopping what she called a 'cab' with one little wiggle of her violet parasol, and by being rich enough to take a taxi for the short distance to the nearest tube station. Down we went together in the lift, enjoying the noises and descent, and miming to one another the delightful and sickening moment when the lift stops but your stomach doesn't. We waited on the hot windy platform till the train roared in, and we sat companionably together on one side of a pair of seats under the bright lights of the swaying carriage. She bent down to catch the comments which my shyness kept below the noise level of the bumping train, and dabbed at her lips with a very small handkerchief edged in violet to match her dress.

I was entrusted with the two green tickets, one full-length and one torn across, and very hot and sticky they got in my clutching hand. I counted the stations as we got to them, marking them off on the map opposite, above the rocking straphangers, until we reached our destination and followed the labyrinth of tunnelled paths to the escalator. On the way up Grandma stood below me, so that her face, bright, lively, smelling of kid leather and patchouli, was surprisingly level with mine. At the theatre we were in the *fauteuils* – the lady attendant called them 'fottles' – and I found the meaning, the pronunciation, and even more the spelling, which I saw at the top of the stairs over the gilded entrance, entirely mysterious. These turned out to be comfortable, high-backed seats of red velvet, towards the back of the circle, and we settled into all the dim-lit excitement of a theatre about to start. I stared at the giant crimson curtain, the shadowy depths of the orchestra pit with the players moving into position, and admired the embossed cover of the programme, my grandma somehow always anticipating and sharing these pleasures.

At the magic moment when the curtain swagged and swayed back, and the orchestra struck up, she held my hand: the opening sequence of brilliantly lit conjuring with its climax of flying doves swirling right over the auditorium was bound up with the feel of my small grubby hand in hers – a soft, warm palm and cold rings on her fingers. Rabbits appeared from impossible places, magic sticks suddenly burst into flame in mid-air, lost five-pound notes reappeared in mysterious circumstances, packs of huge playing-cards rearranged themselves without being touched. Two beautiful assistants in tights and sequins handed things to the two magicians and took on sudden statuesque poses to accompany a roll on the drums and to indicate that applause was now expected. In the interval I felt specially picked out when a silver tray was brought to us with all the impedimenta of afternoon tea, including biscuits on a doily-covered plate. The sense of luxury, as we bit and swallowed and had a second cup, was unforgettable.

I was exhausted with excitement by the time we came out into the early evening sunlight and rode down the escalator into the airless underground. My eyes were heavy while we waited for the train, and when we got in I found it even hotter than on the platform. Soon I dropped off, and was taken into Jenny's arms and happily snuggled, half awake, half asleep, into her soft capacious bosom; I date my lifelong affection for the female torso from that journey. Back in the fresh air I woke up sufficiently to enjoy again the parasol-waving and flagging down of the taxi as it screeched to a halt, the bouncy little journey, and the triumphant arrival at Inverness Terrace. I tried to tell the others what a marvellous afternoon we had spent, but it wouldn't go into words.

During our visit there were a number of grown-up parties at 2 Inverness Terrace. They were very posh, but I never felt patronised and was not at all conscious that any of us were playing the role of poor relation. On the contrary, my father's opinions on art and related matters were elaborately deferred to, while Florence, the adored daughter and only child, was of course everybody's favourite. We quickly began to pretend that the jewels and the wine and the cigars were part of ordinary life.

The evening would start with a lengthy meal. There were two servants, a chunky middle-aged woman and a wispy young thing, both in black-and-white uniform. My grandfather with his white hair apparently freshly shampooed, plump but not fat, moustached but not bearded, smelling of lavender-water and cigars, sat in an upholstered carver at the head of the oval table. Soup came first, or melon pre-cut into bite-sized pieces and decorated with 'glass-cherries'. The napery was thick and starched and the napkins sat up like vultures and had to be dismantled and tucked under the knees at both sides rather than placed on the lap, as they tended to slide off, being both stiff and slippery. The soup was poured from a beautiful silver ladle into our hot deep soup plates, in strict order, I noticed, of ladies, then children, then men, and always from the left. Next was a joint – a vast hunk of beef, a flat huge steaming cylinder of pork, a turkey, a pair of chickens, once a pair of pheasants which were familiar enough to me running across my own Owslebury lanes but something I had never tasted before. Each kind of meat had elaborate accessories: cranberry sauce, red-currant jelly, horse-radish sauce, stuffings of various kinds. The vegetables too were elaborate and varied rather than grossly plentiful – uniform-sized sprouts, small elegant leeks, round identical potatoes roast and boiled, carrots dressed with green sprinklings, cauliflower of creamy elegance in sprigs and covered with a thick smooth white sauce. The puddings were, I thought, the result of even more loving care: trifles consisting of layer after layer of different ingredients – sponge-cake, fruit, custard, nuts, cream – all faintly impregnated with sherry; jellies of various colours – deep green, bright purple, royal crimson, with sauce-boats of cream; pies of very short pastry with smooth and uniform apple looking like greenish mashed potato with, here and there, a black exclamation mark of a clove – which I wasn't sure I liked. These pies were quite different from our home-made product, which were a touch singed at the edges, a trifle stodgy at the centre, with the odd pip or 'toenail' in the firm bits of apple, the crust held up with an inverted eggcup, and the whole served with unquestionably lumpy custard. One evening though, we were offered Queen of Puddings – a delicious mixture of eggs, lemon, breadcrumbs and jam topped with browned soft meringue. This was one of Florence's specialities and an infrequent but particular delight in Owslebury, so I enjoyed doing her culinary justice by observing loudly that her version was every bit as good as the Bayswater one.

However, at Inverness Terrace the food went on: the pudding dishes were swept away by the wispy maid or the chunky one, and bread was served in crusty slices, creamy white butter and a variety of cheeses; then apples, oranges, bananas, grapes – all flawless in comparison with ours. Even *then* they hadn't finished! Walnuts, hazel-nuts and brazil-nuts, nutcrackers, a couple of new dark bottles, coffee in tiny fancy cups, shallow, fluted and gilded: and still the thick damasked tablecloth was spotless except for the crumbs swept away by Wispy with a crumb brush. At last they lit cigars and cigarettes, and even then we children were expected to remain at table at least for a time, while our elders and betters went on swigging and puffing. I looked round at them all, this time without the spectacular distractions of the meal. So how did they look?

Aunt Hilda was a large lady in bottle-green with an enormous mouth, a fine dark skin and small brittle black eyes. She had a strange accent, Scottish I now assume, and a large infectious laugh. Her husband was Frank, and it was well-known that 'Frank drank' – that was the way I remember it – though he didn't seem to me to drink any more than the others who 'drank like fish', an expression I had heard from my father which seemed to me to apply admirably to all of them. Frank was a thin, balding man, rather sarcastic, but with a dry sense of humour which I enjoyed. His sceptical if not cynical attitude to life was not uniform; he endeared himself to me later that evening when, seeing that my seat had been taken while I was upstairs in the lavatory, he pulled me on to his lap for a minute, inviting me as we both sat down to listen to the creaking of his knees – 'You'll be like that when you're my age,' he said, and very impressed I was by this really rather loud noise like a reaper and binder two fields away.

Uncle Ted looked like an overheated horse with a long, long face, and a mouth cluttered with teeth under an absurd walrus moustache which gave him a mournful expression. His nose, chin and the whites of his eyes were cerise; his expression was at once deadened and restive. Tall and potbellied, he was all the same, skinny with veiny hands. He said, 'Oh I say!' too often for my taste and often I wondered what 'Oh I say' meant when it was immediately followed by saying something else. He was regarded by the grown-ups as both rather daring and yet harmlessly 'past it' – mysterious phrases for me with only a dim under-meaning – because, a widower, he lived with his housekeeper, Mrs Royd, in what might conceivably have been sin. Mrs Royd, though reputed by my mother to be very intelligent, was somehow improbable for the role, being enormously fat with a bosom like a vast stuffed sack, and addicted to vivid purple dresses without sleeves. She had mottled arms which were so fat that enough spare flesh hung from the backs of them to hide her elbows. Aunt Grace, to whom I felt very close after the time she and Boughty had visited us in Owslebury, was a more familiar and friendly sight than the others round the table. Comparing her with her neighbours I realised that she had a version of the family face, with the long jaw and big low-slung mouth, but in her case the nervy sadness of expression was relieved by the distant twinkle in her brown eyes. She had 'a sense of humour', and told what everyone obviously considered *risqué* jokes: 'Working man in tube train to middle-aged lady who thinks she is being stared at: "Don't worry, Mum – my hobby's beer!"' (outraged laughter). Boughty didn't have a Christian name as far as I ever discovered; at this party she seemed even older and frailer, and the nervous shake of her head to the left still fascinated me enough to make me try consciously not to stare. She was in a long green evening dress, still hung with jewels, especially on her knobbly arthritic fingers.

After the first round of cigarettes had been stubbed out and people moved from the table to armchairs and sofas, there was a general agreement that the evening's music should begin, and the whole gathering put heavy pressure on Boughty to play the piano, arthritis and all. She protested that she was long past playing well, but was finally persuaded, and launched into three shaky but impressive pieces, all by Chaminade. That composer was then considered the height of classy taste, to be listened to in a breathless hush. ASJ silently flicked his cylinder of cigar ash and looked soulful, Aunt Grace looked proud of her friend, my mother looked exalted, as the knobbly fingers managed, and the banal chords hovered over the whole bright-lit crowd. The heat from the blazing fire hit the middle of my shoulder-blades, the light was a bit dazzling, and on the whole I wanted it to be over.

The soda syphon hissed into several glasses, and then my mother sang 'Three Little Maids from School', accompanying herself, I thought beautifully. Aunt Grace, with Boughty at the piano, sang in a sweet small quaver 'Prithee Pretty Maiden', with its entrancing rhymes:

I would fain discover
If you have a lover

Heigh, willow waley-o!

and even better in the second verse where my pleasure came from what for me was the novelty of two words rhyming with one:

Nobody I care for
Comes a-courting, therefore
Heigh, willow waley-o!

I found this poignant and thrilling. Another favourite was my mother's next song, *A Goldfish Swam in a Deep Glass Bowl*, and the actual taste of its words and rhymes, almost entirely divorced from their meanings, takes me back to the cigar-and-port smells, the clean orderliness everywhere, and my now glowing face set in lines I recognised as happy:

Her small inside he daily fed
With crumbs of the most digestive bread,
'Which kind attention proves,' said she,
'How exceedingly fond he is of me.'

This reminds me that Arthur always thought 'exceedingly' a superior word to 'very', while Florence and Joan preferred 'awfully'.

By this time we were well into the evening's music: we three kids were all sticky with sweets but very attentive in our separate over-stuffed chairs, until Bill, tending to fall asleep, was suddenly whisked off after going the whole vast round of the party to be kissed. Aunt Hilda's son was prevailed upon to sing – handsome Monty who didn't want to be called Uncle and whom I addressed, with a swallow, as Monty. He was clearly younger than most of the party, and regarded as 'brilliant'. They all had permanent labels: Grace was 'a scream', Frank 'drank', and Monty was 'brilliant' (he had a degree), but was not really a bit conceited about it. All characters are expected to keep to their roles, or at least to demonstrate their qualities at regular intervals, like Punch and Judy or Ketch the hangman, and it would have been most confusing if Frank became teetotal or Grace morbid or Monty immodest; they must be frozen perpetually in their predetermined parts. So, with his brilliant white teeth, dark hair and Italian-looking eyes, Monty launched into a bit from *Pagliacci*, accompanied by his mother who played strongly, and it seemed to us, almost professionally. As he sang, especially the *fortissimo* bits, the backs of his trouser legs quivered. Having had this wickedly pointed out to me by Florence, I tried to adopt the right position to see that it did indeed happen. His encore, loudly demanded, was a Hungarian gipsy song done with lots of exciting rhythmic choruses accompanied by piano arpeggios, and another splendid quiver of the trousers.

I think there were duets too, but finally we were told 'Bed-time in twenty minutes for Joan and Peter, and what would they like us all to sing?' So Joan chose from the *Daily Express Community Song Book*, something with plenty of high clear soprano, at which she was a dab, and I opted for the *Three Fishers* who went sailing out into the west, with its touching third verse:

> Three corpses lay out on the shining sands
> On the shining sands as the sun went down!
> And the women are weeping, and wringing their hands
> (high note),
> For those who will never come back to the town.

followed by the chorus subtly modified for the end of the song:

For men must work, and women must weep
And the sooner it's over the sooner to sleep
Tho' the harbour bar be moa-oa-ning . . .

with a delicious moan from us all. This seemed to me to embody a profound and touching truth, and I kept in with my mother who sang her 'seconds' – half alto, half tenor. We finished with the best of all, *Sweet and Low*, which, though sad, ended on a positive note, and by this time an ornamented box of sweets had a lot of empty frilly brown holes where I had been surreptitiously pinching the *petits fours*, and Joan had been stuffing chocolates. We two were paraded for kisses from everyone in the room, and our bedroom with the nightlight and the starched lavender-smelling sheets and the smell of Pears' soap still embodied a blissful novelty contrasting with the apple-hay smell of our Owslebury bedroom. In bed I decided to allot a little time to thinking about Bunty and the three butterflies I'd left on the setting board, but almost instantly sleep obliterated these good intentions.

We arrived home late. Mr Flower's trap from Morestead brought my mother and the three of us, almost asleep, down Jackman's Hill in the cold evening air to the cottage. There was a bustle of unpacking and firelighting and cocoa-making, and soon I was in bed, seeing the bronze moon through the branches of the apple trees just above the mist-covered fields. I was thinking half backwards to the lighted London days, and half forwards to the morning, my Museum and the excitements to come. I could hear the porridge for breakfast being stirred downstairs as I floated off to sleep.

The next morning I woke early. Joan and Bill were both asleep, and outside the world was damp and cold; wisps and tatters of mist lay over the high field, hiding the three thorn trees from view. I put on my oldest trousers and my navy-blue jersey with the floppy collar, and carried my boots down the creaking stairs. The sitting-room was still almost dark, and the whole cottage was chilly after a fortnight without a fire, though Bunty looked happy enough stretched out by the still glowing coals. The bricks were cold to my stockinged feet and I put my boots and jacket on and opened the latch of the front door. The top of the well was dark with wet and there were rows of raindrops along the edges. Through the light mist the apple tree held its ripening red fruits, and I pulled down a twig and held the cold smooth sweetness in my hand. As I bit into it I saw that the pips were going brown. The iron post at the end of the garden was forlorn in waist-high nettles. The swallows gone now, flown to a warmer country, my one Silver-Washed Fritillary *var. valesina* ruined, Tim Hunney dead and the sweet spacious days finished. Sadness settled over me with the melting drops on the branches, the mist on the Medder, the stubbled field in the distance. Only the sparrows were left, it seemed, and I must wait somehow till next March, or February at the very earliest, for the egg season to start again and life to begin. Meanwhile, no doubt, there were still a few flowers to collect, though my pressing-book was full and there was little prospect of another at the moment. But at least I could reorganise my collection of eggs, classify it, make a catalogue. The sparrows chirped around the house-eaves. Soon my mother would be down, and perhaps next time we were in London she might ask Grandpa to take me to the naturalists' shop in London and get some of the things I couldn't ever find – sea bird's eggs, golden plover's, peregrine falcon's – a few of the vast riches of the bird book. Meanwhile I had to get my collection in order.

The Museum was dark, the floor gritty and the shelves dusty. I pushed back the little curtain and let in enough dim light to be able to see the boxes. The two cigar boxes and the cardboard box: there they were, all open; one with silver sand, two with wadding and cotton wool. The faint odour of camphor struck my cold nose. My fingers with my bitten nails, were almost too cold to touch the fragile eggs. It was impossible to label them since labels wouldn't stay in place on cotton wool or sand. Could I perhaps make a drawing and stick it on the lid? I crept into the sitting-room and found the big scissors in the old wicker workbasket by my mother's chair, and in my father's drawer – forbidden territory – I found a roll of paper and cut a piece off.

I drew the first row of eggs to size as near as I could get them: Rook(2), Jackdaw, Jay (addled, but no one would know until they lifted it and found it heavy, and they wouldn't be allowed to do that), Starling, Blackbird, Thrush; Missel Thrush I hadn't got, Raven, and Hooded Crow of course I hadn't. I wrote the names under the egg outlines, squashing the long ones in, hyphenating. Moorhen; Barn-Owl; Coot the next one might be, I thought, but felt a vague dissatisfaction that it was probably an odd Moorhen; Kestrel, badly broken underneath. That was about all the big ones. No Grouse, no sea birds: yes, a Plover from the other box, '*or Lapwing or Peewit*' with the too-soft pencil on the too-soft paper. Great Tit, the one I found in the hollow in Beechy Lane, nest deserted; I hoped it was a Great Tit. Blue Tit, an easy one, came from the holly in Teddy Chenery's garden, one of five eggs in the nest. I wished it was April. The Yellowhammer, from the grass verge down by Mr Gott's, found on a hot morning alone among the cuckoo flowers with Bunty sniffling and getting in the way. Cirl Bunting, might be another Yellowhammer but the book wasn't clear and the eggs looked nearly the same at South Ken. No Coal Tit, no old woods to find it in; no Marsh Tit, none in the marshes. Whinchat, swapped for Federated Malay States stamps, the red 4c and the green 2c. No Swallow – next April in Leslie

Binder's barn. Hawfinch, but might be a big Greenfinch, Linnet easy, Goldfinch, Sparrow easy, Garden Warbler lovely pale green, Whitethroat slightly different lovely olive green. There was another row of eggs – Wren found on Crowe Hill in a pit under the beeches, no Flycatcher, no Redpoll, Hedgesparrow easy, Bullfinch from Schwartz's wood on a cold afternoon keeping look-out for the gamekeeper and seeing a lovely, dead jay with three stoats hanging on a thorn bush like schoolboys caught trespassing; but there was no more room on the paper. Should I perhaps make another strip? But then there was no room to stick it on the lid. Anyway they were badly arranged: waders, birds of prey, warblers, finches, all mixed up in one box. I wondered whether I should take them out and see if they could be rearranged. And then there was the sad box of swaps, some of them perhaps better than the good ones. I put them all out, carefully, on the table. They rolled together in odd-looking clutches . . .

I sighed deeply. Everything was so difficult. There was a movement of bedsprings overhead and feet on the creaking wooden boards. Bunty must be awake, and was nosing at the door. I wondered what time it was. There was more light now through the window. My hands were chilly, the brown apple-core sat inertly on the dusty ledge, the eggs were higgledy-piggledy on the table, and my toes were cold inside the big boots. Now I turned to the swaps and wondered who would want four blackbirds' and five thrushes' eggs. Or the three very different house sparrows' – brown, grey, nearly black, and a yellowhammer not so well marked. And there, under the cardboard sheet of examples of wood – cherry, beech, chestnut – were the butterflies. I thought I would just take a look in case bugs or . . . carefully I lifted down the glass case. The Broad-bordered Yellow Underwing was greasy around the impaling pin, and there were some tiny dots of black under the Red Admiral. I drew off the glass lid and lifted it out by its pin to see again the delicate grey, blue and pink of the underside. I leant to look closer. Only a small, tiny crunch as the corner of the glass leaned against – what was it? Don't let it be the Kestrel, instantaneously, nor, I thought frantically, the Hawfinch, nor . . . I looked. The Swift. And so hard to get; they were so strange and footless, and could only drop from a ledge. Mr Last said put them on the ground and they can't lift themselves. Swift with broken leg dead at Marwell. Broken Swift. Yes. I gathered the bits, my eyes smarting, crossed it off the list, rather savagely, with the too-soft pencil.

Florence heard as I scraped the old chair back on the brick floor, and opened the door.

'You're up early,' she said. 'Aren't you hungry?'

'I had an apple.'

'Porridge is ready,' she said. 'Do you feel like going up to Pooleys to get the milk?'

Might as well. Pretty hopeless. 'Please keep the door shut, mother. My eggs are out. I don't want Bunty in there.'

She looked at me, questioningly, saying nothing.

'I broke one.'

'Oh, Pete – which one?'

'The Swift,' I said brokenly. Then my face was in her skirts.

'I wish we hadn't come home,' I said.

'I'll come with you,' said Florence and then, suddenly and loudly – 'Joan! Bill! Wake up and get up. Joan, make the tea. Pete and I are going for the milk.'

PART FOUR

Autumn, Christmas, Spring

CHAPTER TEN

MAINLY SCHOOL

Some autumn afternoons after school I fed the hens, and they ran through the grass like footballers in long shorts, occasionally taking off for a few yards and squawking with greed or hunger. As I scattered the brown nutshaped grains I thought with pride of the long hours we had spent collecting it, especially as this chicken food was clearly a small, but important contribution to the economy of the cottage, now going through one of its periodic crises. Perhaps the previous high spot of the graph had been higher than usual, or the trough was deeper – or perhaps it was my imagination, as nothing was said, but I noticed that we sold our eggs over the bar of the Shearers, half-dozens in paper bags, instead of eating them. My mother cut her cigarette smoking in half, with some pride and with strong backing from Joan, who was concerned about Florence's cough. My favourite blancmanges and jellies were replaced by perfectly edible but rather monotonous apple puddings, so that the faint daily smell of the pudding cloth and the light slime on the damp suet crust became, and still remains for me, the smell of poverty.

What we much preferred were the plums, also spotted but harmlessly so. Arthur firmly believed that they should be left to ripen, and no amount of evidence would change his mind. But Bill and I saw that wasps and blackbirds also preferred them ripe; they would eat every bit of the inside except the stone and leave sad little flags of purple skin still hanging on the tree. Arthur had strictly forbidden us to climb on the rather crumbly brick coping of the well. But when he was safely in London, and Joan was busy with Florence in the scullery, I broke the law by climbing up, with Bill holding my legs. I put a single boot on the dangerously rotten wooden lid and stretched up high for the paradisal fruits, which I shared with Bill as no more than his due.

We were a bit short of coal and made do mainly with wood, some of which Bill and I proudly chopped and sawed in the barn. Arthur came home only every other weekend. Florence said he was busy in London, and couldn't spare the time.

Our holiday in London meant that we were nearly a fortnight late in starting the autumn term, but we had permission from Mr Last who thought Joan and me capable of catching up quickly with the not very gruelling syllabus. I was engrossed with my new status in the top class at school – above Spud Newton, though he could easily hold me down with one hand – and with the fact that I was now in the same form as Sally Hunney. She always sat on the girls' side and half behind me, alas, so I could rarely steal a glance in her direction. My evenings and weekends were fully occupied with my Museum and a marvellous new book on Butterflies and Moths in four small fat volumes; there were on loan from Mrs Binder, and had belonged to her father. When even I was tired of this, there was the ritual half-hour of reading aloud, when Florence, often reaching for her fag-box but restraining herself most of the time, took us through the long and obscure delights of *The Swiss Family Robinson*.

The daily journey to and from school was coloured by the interesting addition of Bill. It was quickly assumed that since Bill at four and two-thirds would need most of Joan's attention there and back, then I, at the advanced age of seven and a half, must be almost old enough to be able to look after myself. Bill was only apprehensive for a few days and quickly adjusted to the new life; I was pleased to have him round but had two uneasy feelings. First, was it perhaps a pity that Florence was totally alone in the cottage – could Frankie Southgate be trusted to keep his side of the door, and indeed could she be trusted not to smoke too many fags in the absence of filial supervision? Second, surely Bill was too young to be at school: he looked so very small.

In fact Florence had all sorts of elaborate plans, now that the kids were off her hands for some hours daily. She had brought back from London sundry hand-knitted garments 'old but the wool's still good' and she embarked on the endless task of washing, rewinding, and knitting it up again into six-inch squares to make new bedcovers. She was going to get the vegetable garden much more productive; and, improbably but firmly, decided to research the possibility of making cheese out of goats' milk. This last fantasy was obliterated when two of the goats were struck by some obscure, swift and specialised goat disease. In spite of being nursed and fed with a bottle they died, and the infection, whatever it was, struck the rest of our little herd remorselessly. Within a fortnight they were all dead and Frankie was at the cottage, not for dalliance but for the grisly business of skinning and burying, mercifully all done while we three were at school. The pelts were nailed out on the two barn doors, the hairy side next to the door, and attacked with a borrowed fleshing knife by various people, including Arthur. They dried out surprisingly quickly and by midwinter were placed strategically around the bedrooms and sitting-room of the cottage. I think these new rugs were probably undercured because they looked soft but were in fact stiff. They made crimpling noises when trodden on and close up smelled strongly of goat, but we felt that these coarse off-white, grey-and-white and orange-and-white pelts added a touch of rural elegance.

The death of the goats might have been more shattering to me, except that my social focus was beginning to shift from home to school, especially when the autumn grew colder and the older pupils had their lunch standing round the tortoise stove in an enforced intimacy. I began to see individual children much more clearly than in the hot weather, when they had been scattered around the playground and churchyard.

Though I never knew him well or specially liked him, Spud Newton remained an impressive and dominating figure who missed few chances to demonstrate his superiority in most fields except the 'groves of academe', and those he managed to make seem unimportant or even sissy. Conkers was a regular autumn game at school, and Spud produced wrinkled veterans which some of us suspected of having been doctored with vinegar or creosote. 'At's a sixty-three-er, an this 'ere's a nointy-one-er,' he said as he hurled one of them down on its string and my carefully chosen conker, stringed so neatly by my father with a red-hot skewer, lay in pieces while Spud smiled in triumph.

He had a huge sister, Bessy Newton, who had the same colouring but was also fat and spotty, the spots tending to occupy the spaces between the freckles; she had appreciable breasts and a raucous metallic voice generally used for ridiculing somebody or something. She arrived at school one morning with a conspicuous yellow stain down her slightly bumpy front, and when asked about it, she bawled, 'No, 'tain't vaseline, it's egg!' Vaseline was smeared on children in those days for a wide variety of skin blemishes and for things like sties and earaches; but why she thought smeared egg a mark of distinction and a dribble of vaseline commonplace, was obscure to Joan and myself. However, this didn't prevent the phrase from becoming a family tag, used whenever we spilt anything down our fronts. At school she was inseparable from the small dark sly Rosie Lane who lived in Rose Lane which ran alongside the churchyard and faded out into a track. Rosie's body was like a tube, her hair neat, her skin very dark for our village; she was neat verbally as well as physically, easily holding her own when she capped one of Bessy's loud-mouthed jeers with a quiet but clinching comment. Each of the pair seemed a parody of the other, and they looked extraordinary as they walked together down the main road of the village, reminding me of Mutt and Jeff in *Comic Cuts*.

Then there was Bobby Botwright who now became a close friend and joined me when the season began on birdsnesting and butterfly-hunting expeditions. He lived at Baybridge and so was distinguished by having three Bs (or even four). He was the worst nail-biter I knew – and I was expert on this as Joan and I had a continual struggle to stop biting our own, and were familiar with the sensation of a sore and exposed quick at the end of at least one finger. But Bobby had gnawed his down to minute black moon-crescents, and the remnant looked a long way down his finger, with a large pad of flesh which bulged over the little moon-shaped nail. He even chewed the bulge into raw patches. He, too, was dark, and he had scaly eyebrows, small black eyes, leathery skin and a skull of black hair that fitted tightly on his round head over his low forehead and flat-topped ears. His devotion to me moved me deeply. It was the first involuntary, non-family, devotion I had experienced, and I became heavily dependent on him and spent all the spare time I could with him, though we lived a couple of miles apart. As Bobby smelled a bit, and was shy, incoherent and subliterate, my parents preferred the well-groomed middle-class blond boy Leslie Binder who lived near Baybridge too, in a small but rather elegant ex-farmhouse with a fine garden and barns. Leslie was always spotlessly clean, in khaki shirts and trousers which were notably shorter than those of most village boys, and exposed his neat honey-brown knees. His clothes were 'sensible' as well as tidy and unrepaired (most of us had darned socks or pullovers) and he kept himself a little detached from our ruder games and conversations, while never being conspicuously superior.

Most of the children at school were dressed in a way displaced permanently, one hopes, by better rural standards of living, the invention of man-made fibres, and the growing interest in walking and camping. Trouser and jacket material tended to be serge, socks and trousers were very long and almost met, garters were tight, the whole costume a version of that of their farm-working parents who never took off waistcoats or caps until bedtime. A heavy sweat was regarded as the natural outcome of running or even walking fast at any time from May to the end of September. Joan and Bill and I were relatively liberated, but I always wore boots, never shoes. Leslie Binder seemed half-naked by comparison.

In these tranquil days of early autumn the life at school absorbed even more of my interest now that the bird and butterfly seasons were over. There was one bit of high drama which was saved in my eyes from being tragic only by the creeping intervention of a small element of comedy.

One Friday after school I was invited at short notice to tea at a house in the village next door to the Hunney's farm. Two north-country children were staying there with family friends while their mother was in hospital. The Wilkins were an impressive pair, tall, dark, good-looking, energetic; indeed we thought them a bit wild. Joan, preoccupied with getting the rather tearful Bill back home – he had a nosebleed – said I could go so long as I promised to be back home by 5.30 p.m. at the latest. After the tea party there quickly developed an elaborate game of cops and robbers – was it a Carlisle version, I wondered? – which involved chasing not only round most of Owslebury but also many of the surrounding alleys and lanes. It was exciting, and Sally's presence made me bold. We suddenly discovered, or I did, that it was 7.45 p.m. I had no watch and realised too late how long the game had taken. I rushed back home in the soft dusk to find Florence quietly frantic and Joan in tears. I immediately made up a cover story: it was Mr Wilkins, home for the weekend, who had kept us talking and playing games, and – a neat touch, I thought – 'he sent his apologies'. I regretted this the moment I had invented it, but it was too late. Just as I was going to bed Arthur arrived from London for the weekend, found Florence still upset, and ticked me off harshly for being so irresponsible. Next evening, by a disastrous chance, he ran into Mr Wilkins in the village and heard how angry he was that his children were missing for over two hours while those wild and uncontrollable Owslebury kids ramped round the village. Arthur came back very cross indeed.

The family usually took trivial lying easily enough, and each of us often said to the other, 'Oo, you are a fibber!' All the more remarkable was this sudden pernicketiness – and as for being late, that happened often enough, though this was an extreme case. I felt confused and very hard done by. Arthur, his eyes half closed and his stern expression much intensified, held me by the shoulders and stared into my eyes.

'Not content with worrying Your Mother to death by staying out until you're two and a half hours late you then tell her a flat lie. I will not have Your Mother made miserable, but worse is to cover up your own selfish irresponsibility by telling lies. I shall have to thrash you.'

Arthur, very pink, very determined, utterly convinced that he was doing his duty, hunted upstairs for a wide leather belt with a buckle. I was apprehensive indeed but even more I was amazed. I was to be thrashed in the scullery. Unused to this kind of scene, I rushed into the sitting-room and Arthur followed me, shouting.

'You make me hopping mad! You are a little liar and you oblige me to teach you a lesson!' He grabbed me whimpering from the protesting females, dragged me into the other room, and forced me across the table with my wincing bottom more or less uppermost and my bare knees under the cold slab. The first stroke seemed to cut into me through my trousers and my howl was echoed by a moan from Joan in the sitting-room. He struck me hard three times, the third blow cutting across the first, and I tried to wriggle from under his left hand which held the collar of my jersey, and then he said, panting, 'That'll teach you a lesson you won't forget in a hurry. Never let me hear you lying again and frightening your mother and your sister. Now go to bed!'

'No, Florence, Peter is not to be spoiled and cosseted. I will not have this disgraceful behaviour. Get straight up to bed and we'll see if we can forget it in the morning.' Still crying I looked at Joan and my mother without speaking and took my shaking legs and my stinging rear up the stairs, undressed in the dark and crept in alongside Bill.

Gradually the pain diminished and I was beginning to think I could get to sleep when I heard slow steps up the stairway, and woke thoroughly in the hope that Florence had been allowed to come and say goodnight. The door opened and a tray appeared with a lighted candle on it and behind it Arthur. He put it down on the chair by my bed. It had on it, amazingly, two thick doorsteps of toast with Florence's apricot jam, and a mug of hot, steaming cocoa. Sore and a bit outraged though I was, I couldn't help finding his appearance a trifle funny.

'I'm sorry I had to thrash you, old man,' he said rather brokenly. 'I did it for your good. It hurt me', he added with enormous conviction, 'more than it hurt you.' My flaming bottom under the bedclothes doubted this, but he kissed me through my last faint sobs, half ashamed, it seemed, of his fury.

Licking the last remnants of jam from my lips I fell asleep thinking of Sally Hunney. How Bill slept through all this I don't know, but he didn't stir, and as far as I know wasn't ever let into the secret of my disgrace. I didn't manage to feel guilty at any point, albeit sore and a bit outraged – but this was on a diminishing scale. The lesson I was supposed to have been taught remained obscure, but I was careful thereafter for some weeks not to 'rub Daddy up the wrong way'.

The impressive but disturbing Wilkins children soon returned to Carlisle, and at school we settled back into routine activities. All the outliers, and some of the village children, brought our own lunch to eat at school, and in winter gathered round the tortoise stove to cook cheese, toast bread and warm our hands. The stove was surrounded by a brass fireguard and for half the morning was topped with a vast kettle in which Miss Gorman made cocoa for us in a two-handled teapot. It was poured into our own enamel mugs and we added our own sugar and milk brought daily in screw-top jars. We made up our special cliques and refused to speak to rivals: 'They're not speaking' was a newsworthy indication of the state of classroom politics. The inseparable Bessy and Rosie queened it over these sessions, and gathered a little court around them, usually close to the stove, thus leaving those of us not currently favoured by their approval out in the cold. There was gross superstition on many topics, and we were all continually expecting disaster or wild success because of the behaviour of cats or owls or the moon. Everyone fervently believed that it was unsafe to leave out metal objects like knives and forks during a thunderstorm, as they 'drew' the lightning. There was, of course, a great deal of gossip about adults; someone had had twins and nearly died at Bishop's Waltham hospital. Bessie claimed to know all about this, but most of us had only the haziest idea about birth and there was a widespread conviction, which Bobby Botwright firmly shared, that the baby came out of the belly-button. I knew about the umbilical cord, having once seen it clearly during the birth of a calf, but as cows had no belly-buttons the matter remained confusing.

There was a small, cross-looking and slightly cross-eyed little girl called Dotty Tranter. She frequently had a snivelly cold and her pinafore was often grubby. One cold lunch-time we were again talking about sex round the stove when Dotty, who was not a leading conversationalist said, 'My grandpa does it to me sometimes'. We were astonished rather than horrified and asked her to tell us more. 'It's when me Dad's up The Ship in the evenins. E ses to me, "What about a bit?" An e sits me on is lap and puts it in. He gives me sweets then, allus the same – peardrops. An when I see the bag on the side I reckn e'll arsk me agin. I don mind. It don matter to me, an it don take long. Yeh, that's what e ses to me, e ses, "What about a bit?" When e puts it in it don't urt now, notatall. An I git all them peardrops.' The matter was not discussed, and I think those of us who had seen the very old whiskery Mr Tranter senior, as well as the unappealing Dotty herself, considered it a trifle squalid. All the same I was glad that Joan was in the other room helping with the littleun's lunches.

We seemed to take a morbid interest in one another's physical ailments: grazes, cuts, wounds, were displayed by lifting the sticking plaster or shifting the bandages, and a large one was duly admired. Sometimes the wound 'stuck' to the dressing – this was considered by all as a matter of fate; if it happened the dressing had to be painfully loosened with hot water dabbed on the edges, and released bit by bit by pulling. Sometimes, again, a graze or cut would be said to be 'gathering' – becoming infected – and this also was a small mark of distinction, like losing a leg.

I remember feeling very strange one afternoon at school; Miss Gorman's kind downy face grew by turns bigger and smaller. I was wrapped up well and taken home with bossy care and much clucking by Joan who said several times on the surprisingly long journey that I looked flushed. I was put straight to bed on the sofa, and given a stone hot-water bottle with an uncomfortable stopper. The only memory of the illness was the sensation that all the soft things – the pillow, the blankets, my mother's hand – had gone hard as stone. For a few hours I was frightened, but soon I was back at school again. There were grisly tales about toothache round the stove at lunch-time, and indeed a general terror of the dentist, particularly the once-a-year school dentist, who had bad breath and was widely believed to be always drunk; children would bring notes from parents to refuse his attentions. One boy, called Cooper, had two thumbs on one hand – the extra one, rather vestigial, sprouting from the side, and he could hold a scrap of paper between them, which we often persuaded him to do. He was a nail-biter too, and bit all eleven of them.

One November lunch-time we were gathered as usual round the school stove when some children arrived red-nosed from the playground shouting excitedly, 'It's reely gittin foggy out there!' 'Can't ardly see the church even!' 'Come an ave a look!' So we did, and found ourselves instantly in a creamy-white and empty world. We could just see the houses across the road, but they were merely a darker grey than the surrounding air instead of the usual vivid red, grey and brown of their brick, flint, and thatch. This was my first real fog and made even more difference to the look of the village street than snow. Inside the lamps were lit before afternoon school started, and half-way through the first lesson Mr Last left us to 'get on' by ourselves, and then surprisingly returned leading a crocodile of the littleuns, including a slightly bewildered-looking Bill. When we were all assembled he said that there was a rather thick fog which might possibly get worse, 'So I am closing the school – Be *quiet*, Botwright – I know you're excited at being able to miss some lessons. The village children will have no problems but should get straight home. The pupils from further off should start on their journeys home in case it gets thicker. You must keep together and not wander about and get lost. There is nothing to worry about,' he added, looking at the ranks of mostly excited faces, 'and we shall all meet at the usual time tomorrow when the wind will have blown the fog away. Be sensible and don't run in case you run into something and hurt yourselves.' So we quickly packed satchels and put on our coats, hats, scarves, mittens, and amid excited squeaks and mock farewells we left the others and launched out into the amazingly changed world. The wall of whitish fog, obliterating vision, was damp and cold and we had the sensation of plunging into it. 'No, *of course* we can't go by the footpath, Bill – we'd get lost.' Joan firmly demanded that as Mr Last had told us to keep together, we should hold hands. This we flatly refused to do, so she had to settle for one of us on each side of her and thus we remained in touch.

On the corner of Crabbe's Hill a large cart separated us for a little while and gave me time to whisper to the excited and fog-struck Bill, and gang up with him in a small way I wasn't proud of later. As we began to go downhill our feet didn't find the road as soon as we expected; it was an odd sensation. Half-way down Bill suddenly said, 'I've dropped my cap' and paused to retrieve it, while Joan and I went on a couple of paces. This gave Bill time to jump or scramble up on to the steep bank where he must have stood totally still, if not actually holding his breath. Joan left my side and panted uphill to where she thought he had stooped down for his cap – but no Bill! As soon as she left me I ran two or three yards through the thick fog, the dense leaves muffling my footsteps, and climbed with some difficulty off the hard road surface and up on to the softer bank, where I clung to an invisible cold wet sapling for support. Discovering that I too had vanished Joan quickly became frantic and we could hear her running, or at least floundering, up and down that bit of the hill and even across it to the far side, shouting and calling out. I held my pose for a minute or two until her increasingly anguished tones suddenly no longer seemed funny. It had seemed a good joke, but it had turned sour. I jumped down into her path, nearly bowling her over. 'It's all right, Joan,' I cried. 'We were only fooling about.' Bill, back on the road surface, shouted, 'Ever been had?' Joan reached him, shook him, and swore she would report us to Florence 'for frightening the life out of me, you little *beasts*!' She got hold of both of us somehow. 'And now you *will* hold hands, both of you, and don't you dare let go!'

We grunted apologies, held on tightly mitten to mitten one on each side, and soon came out from the tunnel of trees into the marginally lighter air by the Pooleys. Here I was required to take the lead and walk actually in the little ditch, using my left foot to scrape the edge and thus keep us to the road. The footing was slippery and the long dead grasses stroked my socks and quickly soaked them; but we managed to move forward in a backward-stretching row, still holding on mitten-to-mitten, which at this angle made progress very slow. Joan trod on my heels and Bill on Joan's, the structure of the threesome near a farce. Thus we groped our way to the dripping wet front gate. Bill and I were relieved to see, pinned on the front door, a message in Florence's amazing rococo handwriting, 'Had to go over to Chenery's. Back soon.' Very soon she arrived and said, 'It's so thick out there you can't see your hand in front of your face! You must have been let out early. I was just thinking I'd have to come and fetch you. I might have missed you on the way. Well done, Joan! Was it awful?' We thought it a mark of real restraint if not nobility when Joan showed that she had calmed down enough not only to forgive us but not to tell on us. We whispered thanks and apologies as soon as Florence went into the scullery to prepare an early supper for us all.

Apart from unusual days like that one, school continued on a regular pattern, and each school day was enclosed by the journey with Joan and later with Bill as well. As we lived a mile away – at least by road – this made us a bit alien to the children who lived near the school and church, and we felt a tension between the socialised absorbing life of the school and the far-off cottage which contained everything we really loved. In term-time we set off from home with our lunch in canvas satchels, walked by road to Pooleys' farm, and then up a steep footpath over a quarter-mile of rough pasture flanked by the belt of woodland where we played Red Indians. Joan usually got us there on time, though I can remember tearing my grey trousers on the stile that led through the farmyard into the village street, and having to endure the shame of a ragged trouser leg throughout the school day. Occasionally when it was very wet or snowy we would go 'the long way' round Crabbe's Hill, as we always did on the way to church. The trudge home was pleasing even after a day interspersed with long and dangerous slides in the playground, and Florence would sometimes come and meet us, and perhaps if we were flush with money, take us into Cobbs' on the way home for sweets. It was already enchantingly lighted with lamps, which made it a dramatic contrast from the darkening village street, and even more so when, coming out again, we found that in spite of appearances from inside, it still wasn't pitch-dark outside.

CHAPTER ELEVEN

A COTTAGE CHRISTMAS

In those days the commercial Christmas didn't start till December, and when it did the familiar displays of Cobbs' shop were transformed. Cobbs' Christmas goodies were utterly distinct from the presents which Grandpa and Grandma Jennings sent us from London. Unlike those remote, glamorous and expensive things, the offerings behind the misted-over window of the shop were accessible throughout the season, but unobtainable because we couldn't afford them. Being in Cobbs' with Florence sharpened my lust for these dazzling but deplorable manufactured objects – though perhaps 'dazzling' isn't quite the word for a colour scheme of pale pink, dull brown and watery blue. The manufactured stockings were backed with cardboard and fronted with white netting with lots of pink paper packing which insulated the objects from one another. A very large stocking was 6s. 3d., a huge one 14s. 6d. With the wilfulness of childhood it was these and their contents that I fancied – a taste often beyond my parents' means and outside my grandparents' knowledge – typical wares of the isolated village shop and the back streets of small towns.

It's a long time since I saw these Christmas stockings and I have to think hard to remember the contents. Among the seasonal offerings there were always some Japanese water flowers, of which we always had several packets; the covers or folders were beautifully and minutely made, and illustrated with pictures of glamorous panicles and trusses of multicoloured flowers. Inside were delicate slivers that looked like lilliputian slices of cucumber and overcooked beetroot, white in the centre, red at the edges; you were instructed to float them in water, and when you did so they slowly opened up and changed into somewhat larger but otherwise identical slices of beetroot and cucumber, but with vague grey tentacles lying on the water's surface. There were never more than two colours but I was foxed by the beautiful package, and felt that Christmas was incomplete without a saucer of these funny little objects to stare at. Then there were the tiny books of twelve or sixteen pages, held by a single staple and printed on paper in which were embedded slivers of straw and chaff; they were usually highly moral in tone, with blue, pink and black illustrations on the front cover and an advertisement for Iron Jelloids or Dr Collins' Chlorodyne Cough Mixture on the back. These little booklets charmed me mainly by their smallness; the stories themselves were disappointingly flat and dull. There were countless objects in pink tissue paper, either as part of the made-up 'Xmas Stockings' or separate, with a paper label stuck on the front. Inside might be Dolly's Scales made of bright tin, minute cutlery in soft shiny metal which bent only too easily, little plates with joints of meat made of some plastery substance dabbed with red and white paint; comic noses or moustaches or spectacles with moveable eyeballs; magnets with little rods to pull about; metal puzzles made of two convoluted heavy-wire structures which had to be separated – these I remember, always fastened with cotton on to a card which claimed that their possession would make you the Life and Soul of any Party, Hours of Fascinating Fun; conjuring tricks – the Vanishing Ball, the Magic Ring (cast in lead I think, or solder), amputated fingers with realistic nails and bloody bandages, and Magic Jokes depending on covering someone's face with soot or persuading them to light noisy or explosive fake cigarettes. Even the most futile aspects of this seasonal industry delighted me: a pound note printed on rubber – He makes his Money Stretch a Long Way – sheets of perforated sticky-backed 'scraps' with Christmas themes, flat little charms made at that time of metal or glass. Shutting the door on the brightly lit shop and coming out into the cold street we quickly forgot the expensive delights within, especially when Joan struck up a carol we had sung that very morning accompanied by the wheezy harmonium at school, and we all joined in down Crabbe's Hill in the pitch-blackness and through the tunnel at the bottom still faintly lit by the last moments of the sunset.

School broke up for the Christmas holidays in a blaze of subdued glory with pale pink and blue streamers and paper chains suspended between the gaslamps and the varnished picture rails of the big classroom. Holly and ivy were propped and balanced behind the sepia-coloured school-group photos on the walls, and Spud Newton, Sally Hunney, Bobby Botwright, Leslie Binder and the others, all broke up in loving-kindness tinged with excitement, to disappear for nearly three weeks into their infinitely distant houses; down lanes, across icy fields – even into the next parish. At this time of year we would be unlikely to meet till next term, and in our little settlement of Owslebury Bottom the family felt cosily cut off from the ordinary channels of life – to be visited, perhaps, but not on the whole to stir ourselves outside the small area, especially if we were lucky enough to have some snow.

When I walked up the ice-crackling road to the farm for our morning milk, the dawn sky was red, smudged with restless cloud movements, but the thrush on the very top of the leafless ash tree sang bravely enough against the wind. I was full of Christmas excitement and anticipation: again and again my mind settled on to the big white-wooded hamper from the London store, Kearley and Tong's, that had been sent by our grandparents and was waiting in the barn till Christmas morning. The clean white wood contrasted with everything dark and worn in the barn, and the hamper shone like a light in my imagination – not only for its contents, but for itself – the neat studding of the bright-headed nails, the three tacked-on labels, the stencilled letters of the firm's name. Separately, sitting on the top of the hamper, were postal packages even more mysterious and desirable, in stuck-down brown paper; presents from relatives and friends, some for the whole family, but most of them for the three children. One particular package addressed to Bill in Aunt Grace's elegant italic handwriting produced some avid discussions with him about its contents, which we tried to guess from its weight, shape, size and the rattle or padded muffle it produced when we surreptitiously shook it. I found this a pleasant speculation, but the parcels I really passionately cared about were the ones addressed to me. One was obviously a book, but the one I most wanted to open was labelled 'WITH GREAT CARE: From Watkins and Doncaster, 36 The Strand, London, WC2.' I knew it contained butterflies – would they have survived the postal bashing? As I trudged along in the cold I tried to picture what was inside this package. Which of the marvellous butterflies unobtainable in my two square miles of Hampshire would be pinned there, mute and beautiful? I went in my imagination from the warm sitting-room to the cold scullery and through the latched door to the icy barn, and fingered the long thin box of butterflies. The milk ladled into my can was warmish and the farm smelled of hay and woodsmoke, but the can handle felt cold to my mittened fingers as I retraced my steps.

Then, two days before Christmas, Joan and I had a morning collecting greenery. We always found plenty of well-berried holly which was too springy to sit in the pram without jostling itself out again, and all the ivy we could want from the big trees by Pooleys', though you had to be careful and witty-fingered to get a long climbing trail off without snapping it across. I hoped against hope for mistletoe which I never found in Hampshire, perhaps because I obstinately believed that it really preferred oak as a host, and always expected to find a great swag hanging from the branch of any oak tree I passed. Still, collecting the Christmas decorations made a lovely pursuit in spite of cold feet and cold fingers, and as we struggled to get the pram over the icy ruts of the field paths the first big flakes of snow began to fall. The leaves of our proud collection looked gloriously festive when we nailed and fastened them up. There was a special excitement in displaying these branches and twigs in our hot little sitting-room after their long period out in the cold windy woods.

Christmas morning started very early. Bill woke first, and then I, but only Joan was allowed to light the candle. So until she woke, Bill and I lay in breathless excitement in the dark room, looking to the little window, savouring the mysterious sensation of being awake in the middle of the night – though the cocks crowed coldly out of the blackness and told us that the day had really begun. We discussed the dim shape of the stockings hung one each side of the end rail of the bed, and padded out together on the cold boards to stare at the snow, sulphuric blue against the lowering indigo of the night sky, cold and peerless and still with a kind of finality. The hawthorn hedge and the three trees at the back of the meadow, blackly defined, were the only things that made the landscape recognisable as our own. The cold got at our ankles and round our waists under our pyjama tops, and we ran back to bed, not forgetting to squeeze our stockings on the way, hoping to detect their contents, but we felt only the paper which concealed unrecognisable shapes, and the familiar apple like a great loose toe at the very bottom.

Still, we contrived to make enough noise to wake Joan, who lit the candle, put on a rather astonishing orange bed-jacket, and was terribly nice and a bit indulgent about our presents. She made us clear up our piles of paper afterwards, while she opened her own stocking, and seemed to know, to our mystification, about most of the contents. The bleak but strong light was by this time beginning to square off the window, and down we all went, clothes bundled in our arms and taking great care not to make a noise. Some of the loose elm treads creaked loudly in spite of our care, but we let down the latch of the door at the stair bottom very gently, and so into the sitting-room, slightly fusty after the smoking that had gone on there the previous night. Before the candle came down into the room in Joan's hand, we could see the fire still glowing behind the bars, though in full candlelight it looked grey and dead. We put a little bundle of twigs on it from the box and then raked it out, and soon it was spluttering and flaming. Joan moved the porridge pot over to make room, and put the big black iron kettle on the trivet. The table had a blanket over it and was covered in exciting and mysterious bumps, which Joan forbade us even to feel. We dressed by the glowing fire, poured out cups of tea on the hearth, sugared them, and carried them carefully up the staircase with a good deal of creaking and shushing, and into the bedroom to wake our parents and shout 'Happy Christmas!' My mother, I thought, had been awake for some time, but played possum, not wanting to spoil our treat.

Soon after this we were allowed to open our 'main' presents, from our parents and local friends, though not the ones that had come through the post, which had to wait till after breakfast. There was a great deal of toing and froing up and down stairs, with Joan's new doll, a stencil set for each of us, a bag of toffees, a home-made drawing-book. My chief present was a packet of 1000 different stamps – 'All the World' it was labelled proudly – with a transparent panel to show the mysteries within, and I was thrilled to think of the sets I would stick in my album. That morning Joan and I went together to get the milk. Our footsteps, instead of ringing out as usual, were muffled, and the little road was transformed by the snowfall; the ash tree had snow lodged in the forks, and there was snow balanced on every twig in the hedgerows. All was still and quiet, the road so little marked that we could follow our own footsteps in reverse on the way back. In spite of the snow Havertons' yard was muddy with the cows' trampling, and they breathed cloudily over the wall. Mrs Pooley gave us a big bag of walnuts and some beautiful yellow apples as Christmas presents from the dairy farm. When we got back, pink-nosed and tingle-fingered, the double-saucepan of porridge was steaming gently. My father, I believe, not shaved for once, was sitting at the table, the big lamp out. The wintry light struck through the little windows and on to Bill's entranced face as he stared at the three coloured balloons hung from the bacon hook in the corner of the ceiling.

Christmas breakfast was special, as the cliffy porridge we survived on for most of the year was followed by two boiled eggs each, and toast. Florence boiled the eggs, and as she knew that none of us could bear runny white she always overcooked them. The price we paid for a stiff opaque white when we took the top off was usually a crumbly and unexciting yolk, which made difficulties as we were supposed to dip fingers of toast into it. Joan toasted the bread with a fork balanced against the trivet. She chose this moment to distribute the unopened Christmas cards by each plate (for some reason they were saved till after breakfast) and a couple of times she let out little shrieks to indicate that the smell of charring had just reached her. We had a jolly meal, but my heart was beating at the thought of the Watkins and

Doncaster package, and I had difficulty in not bolting my last mouthfuls of toast topped with orange slivers of home-made marmalade. Then the moment came. After the cards had been opened and the breakfast cleared away it was agreed by my parents, aiming I think at a combination of discipline and compassion, and endorsed by Joan, who had a coalition with them in such matters, that the little ones couldn't be expected to wait until all the housework was done before we saw what Aunt Grace had sent Bill and what ASJ had sent me. So Bill got his rectangular parcel and I my long thin one. With a self-restraint I felt proud of – but after all it was the season of goodwill – I helped Bill get off the brown paper which was stuck down so thoroughly with sticky waterproof strips that Aunt Grace might have designed it to keep dry for a fortnight or so in the sea. Inside was a fabulous little train set made entirely of pale wood. The box was endearingly divided into separate compartments for the two locomotives, the tender, the goods carriages and the passenger coaches. There were no rails but Bill was entranced, and he fastened the whole lot together with the tiny hooks and eyes and ran it round the table top, until I reminded him that now it really was my turn.

The butterfly parcel was packed so beautifully that my father opened it for me, perhaps to reward me for my unselfishness with Bill, perhaps because it really was too tricky for me. The wrappings off, a long wooden box was exposed, beautifully finished and varnished except where the lid fitted tightly over the projections of the box itself. I lifted it with some difficulty and all our heads bent over to see the contents. Twelve butterflies, exquisite and contrasting. A Dark Green Fritillary showed the underside (exactly what I had asked for), the forewings a fulvous brown dabbed with black, and moss-green overlying primrose on the hind wings. Next to it was a Comma, its brown wings indented like any

November leaf. Then came a Marbled White, an inch and a half of white on black, or indeed black on white: 'It's really a Brown,' I said with a hint of superior knowledge, and the remark was so manifestly absurd that my parents looked a bit incredulous though they knew 'Peter was clever'. Best of all, perhaps, was a variety of the Clouded Yellow called *helice* – grey and black spotted with yellow – a thing I had loved, longed for and stared at so often in the book. At the end of the box there was room for the last pair of butterflies to be pinned side by side, they were so tiny: a Bedford Blue, a mere scrap of grey with a hint of blue, and a Chequered Skipper to go with my home-killed Dingy and Grizzled Skippers. All had their proper complement of antennae and all were labelled with names and places of origin. Even the Bedford Blue, the smallest of British butterflies, had a confetti-sized bit of pasteboard under the pin, on which was written – surely with the aid of a magnifying glass – 'Crewkerne: May 1919'. So much pleasure, so much fulfilment! I took the box tenderly into the museum.

After we had all shared the housework and had decided that the roads were a bit dangerous for church, we had instead the ritual opening of the hamper from Kearley and Tong's. Arthur took over this exciting job as the nails were regarded as dangerous for children. It was done in the barn to avoid the mess of straw packing and woodshavings, and once my father had pulled out the long silver-shining nails from the lid with the claw end of the hammer and got the twisty metal strip off, the three of us were allowed to take a lucky dip in turn and bring new treasures to light. These were brushed down and then carried into the scullery where my mother admired them and piled them up. It struck me as strange and curious that inside the whitewood packing-case should be a number of smaller whitewood boxes. The first we took out contained hazel-nut creams, strawberry-coloured cones with a nut on the top, pink and uniform in tiny frills, and three layers divided by lace-paper; for me these embodied the once-a-year richness of Christmas. By their necks we pulled out two bottles, one octagonal in section, one in a straw overcoat. There were tins of various luxuries; crystallised fruits, a small Christmas pudding topped with a sprig of artificial holly, cigars of two charmingly different sizes in cedarwood boxes with gilt fleur-de-lis fastenings – perfect for birds' eggs, as I quietly registered to myself. Still the hamper was only half empty. There were two circular tins of cigarettes labelled with a portrait, I thought, of George V in sailor's uniform; a gaudy cardboard box of crackers, a fat-bellied grey jar of ginger netted with wickerwork, chocolates in a padded box with crimson ribbon tastefully bowed, a boat-shaped box of dates, shelled nuts and raisins in two bags like tiny sacks. Then, surely, we had finished, but at the very bottom we found a heavy brown ham smelling of grocers and spices and brown sugar, which specially delighted my mother and would go so well with the cold chicken on Boxing Day. I groped round the straw and sawdust at the bottom; then Bill climbed in to see if he could find anything else, and Joan said he was a little pig, and wasn't he ever satisfied? Back in the scullery Florence said to Arthur, 'Not a penny short of ten pounds – they really shouldn't!' in deprecating tones, though I could see that she was flushed and delighted at the Arabian Nights look of the scullery table.

We admired the piled-up products of our labours, and then we were sent out to find our traditional Christmas flowers. They made an interesting contrast to the metropolitan splendours we had been handling for the past half-hour. Even in the snow we found a rather cankered and despondent-looking rose, two wilted heads of ragwort from a protected corner, a few frost-blasted but still pink heads of lesser deadnettle. Then there was nothing to stop my going back to my cold Museum to gloat again over my album and my stamp mounts and my packet of a thousand stamps – a thousand, think of it! – and the 1920 catalogue with the crude little woodcuts to identify them. Bill sat beside me with his thinner and smaller album; he was to have only duplicates, my father had insisted, as (a) he was younger, and (b) the stamps were my Christmas present. I started off in fine form with dozens of unused stamps that I hadn't ever seen. Poland, Hungary, Russia and above all Germany, had made some revenue by selling sheets of inflation issues to stamp dealers: and so from 3 marks we went to 30 marks and then to 300. They made up beautiful sets but you had to be careful not to dampen the gum or they would be irrevocably stuck down in the album. Again I was haunted and dazzled by plenitude; and again as more and more stamps went into the album I began to be more and more despondent as Bill got absolutely nothing. So I started to cheat quietly, and give him stamps which I knew to be different but which looked rather like the ones I already had. My own cupidity prevented me from doing this very often, and it was my father, after all, who had insisted that this should be the rigid rule, but it was I who in the end burst into tears and had to be comforted, and decided that I just wouldn't collect Finland at all, and gave him the lot, when Arthur wasn't looking. This unhappiness, however, deep though it was, was not allowed to last long, with the delicious smells of roasting chicken and stuffing and hot mince-pies, and my father smoking his first Christmas cigar by the fire. Then we laid the table, put a scarlet and gold cracker by each plate, and fastened up the paperchains that had come loose, while my parents went over to the pub to wish the Chenerys a Happy Christmas. They came back smelling of sherry, my mother with a glow in her eyes and a tendency to giggle.

After dinner I was given the job of clearing up the considerable scatter of fragments left over after the luxurious pulling of crackers. The paper hats I put aside for later use, but the rest seemed to me far too good to burn and as I collected together the decorative 'scraps', the bits of red and gold crêpe, the exploded strips with the burnt ends, the discarded mottos and minute celluloid gifts, the latter kept if they weren't already broken, I was a bit saddened at the thought of all that glory so soon over. Perhaps an overfull stomach caused this passing sadness.

A long languid period followed while my parents slept off their meal. Joan and I read our new books and Bill stencilled vigorously and inaccurately at the table. When she was tired of reading, Joan started dressing and undressing a cardboard doll with cardboard clothing. Then we stumped through the snowy grass in the fading light to feed grain to the chickens, and back to the muggy little room with the glowing fire, feeling torpid and sticky after the hours of eating – figs and nuts and sweets and chocolate. Tea seemed a bit redundant, but we manfully ate bread and jam and lit candles on the Christmas cake and put on our paper hats again – my father was still a king in a green crown. We relit the brass lamp with some difficulty, as it always smoked, and helped wash up. Then we sang carols, my mother putting in arbitrary but pure 'seconds' as she called them, in her light contralto, and my cup of happiness was full.

When at last we got up the creaking stairs with our cups of water and our candles it seemed a good time for a long rhapsodic talk with Bill – but somehow we were too drowsy and the day had been too perfect for comment. We could hear the clock ticking, the fire crackling, and laughter from downstairs. A tawny owl called coldly far away beyond Farmer Gale's cottage and the Field of the Runcible Cow. As I fell asleep, my usual apple only half-eaten, I reflected cosily that even such a day as this wasn't all, and that tomorrow was

Boxing Day with similar pleasures and some new ones, including the rearrangement of my butterflies. I drifted off thinking for the hundredth time of my dusted grey, black-edged, chrome-spotted beauty, the Clouded Yellow, *Colias edusa var. helice.*

CHAPTER TWELVE

SPRING IN THE VALLEY

On another short visit to London we spent a Sunday at my father's parents' house in Dulwich. It was a tiny but detached house with a step of gleaming whiteness and pots on the outside ledge of the bay window in which fuschias were grown in the summer. It had a miniscule back garden imprisoned in neat creosoted fencing on three sides. The last time I had seen it was the previous summer; then it was ablaze with annuals – yellow-pouched calceolarias, white margeurites regarded with special affection as they shared their name with my mother's middle one, blue hammocks of lobelia interspersed with white alyssum, and some apple-pink fleshy-stemmed balsams – the first, and almost the last time I ever saw them. The plants were regimented so closely that scarcely an inch of the soil was visible, and the whole effect was a bit like the view through my recently acquired kaleidoscope. But now the beds were empty and damp and raked into stoneless uniformity, and the grass edges looked as though they had been trimmed with nail-scissors.

My grandfather greeted us at the door: his name was George, but this was never used, as he was called Father by his wife and Dad by his children. I thought him immensely old; he was slow-moving, slow-breathing, large-bellied, bald, with small eyes underlined by conspicuous baggy pouches, and had a long white beard and a white moustache, stained orange by a pipe, although he seldom seemed to smoke. He boasted that he had never shaved in his life. He was dressed, as always, in black and a white shirt and large fanatically polished black boots. *His* father was distinguished in family lore for having been Constable of the Close at Norwich Cathedral, and George had been born on a bridge (Pools Ferry in Norwich) which few, surely, could claim. Grandma I had no reservations about. She was tiny – not all that much bigger than me; tiny and deeply wrinkled on every inch of her soft face and neck, with scorings like nearly parallel contour lines. Her bunned hair, very wide in the parting, was almost as thin as her husband's, and I was a bit incredulous when she said that she 'used to be able to sit on it'. Her maiden name was Polly Strike, and a family joke was to repeat the entry from her class register when she was a child: 'Beryl Baggs, Gwendolyn Slapcabbage, Polly Strike . . .' She wore a Queen Alexandra type of high-necked dress, always black, and her jewellery was also black, made I understood of jet. She was gentle, sweet, and surprisingly witty, and I was told later than although Grandpa went 'religiously' to church every Sunday morning she remained an implacable agnostic and so, conveniently, stayed at home to cook the Sunday dinner.

Grandpa was a retired joiner, and beautiful examples of his work – a sideboard, a table, a carver chair – occupied every spare inch of floor space not filled by large members of the family. He adored his minute wife and allowed her to decide virtually everything, while she pretended deference to him as the Great Male. There were lots of children of the marriage – and here were some of them – Jack, George, Arthur (my father), Annie, Lily and Beatie. Beatie was the oldest and one of the most memorable, because she lived at home, being stone deaf and having never married. She taught me to speak to her a little on my fingers, and I had also to write her interminable messages on little pads of scrap-paper which she kept for the purpose. She handed me a silvery pencil on a long fine silver chain fastened to her waist so I got close to her camphory smell when I was writing her messages. She had been deaf since the age of twelve, and had developed a strange way of speaking. When we were all having third helpings at dinner she was famous for saying 'Not any more, thank you' in an intonation we could all imitate, and she apparently believed that 'films' were pronounced 'flims', which mystified and fascinated me. So did the half-rhyme of her name, 'Auntie Beatie'. She was farmed out for short periods to relatives, presumably to give her parents a rest, and once or twice we found her ensconsed at Uncle Jack's or Auntie Lily's when we visited there. She was regarded by all as noble, worth helping, pitiable, and 'a bit of a trial'.

Uncle Ben was someone's husband, and an undertaker, but today he was in pale grey. He had a large blank face, a neat small moustache, and the kind of thick glasses which make the eyes disproportionately huge and pale seen from the front. He was sitting squeezed in the corner where an aspidistra on a stand tickled his neck, drinking bottled beer with the wonderful cockney Bert (someone else's husband) who worked at Covent Garden with Fred, and who, like Uncle Frank, drank. Everyone kissed everyone, an orgy of kissing, while our tiny Grandma appeared from the kitchen and greeted us with her gold-rimmed glasses steamed over and her usually pallid face a delicate pink, a small wrinkled patch of which she offered me to kiss. Soon Ben and Bert were laying the meal and setting out a small table for Joan, Bill and myself, placed in the only possible area and yet exactly where everyone trying to get to the kitchen was certain to trip over it. Grandpa took off his black tie for lunch and this meant taking off his stiff collar too and replacing the stud at the top of the shirt; still, the beard hid most of it. He sat at the head of the table flanked at the outset by the impassive Auntie Beatie and later by his birdlike and fidgety wife, and sharpened the well-honed knife on a weird-shaped stone before he carved the large joint. Children were served first in this household, with such questions as 'You like outside, don't you Peter?' and 'A little fat for Joan?' at which she visibly shuddered towards me and said, 'Just a little'. As he carved a neat plateful it was passed to the kitchen for vegetables, with Ben and Bert as the Charlie Chaplins of the conveyor belt and Grandma at the far end helped by my mother. Two preconditions had to be carried out before anyone got a mouthful: first, when we were reseated Grandpa looked sternly and slowly once round the table, closed his eyes, and said, 'For what we are about to receive may the Lord make us truly thankful for Jesus Chrissake,' and we all intoned 'Amen'. Then Bert leapt to his feet again to open the bottled beer and everyone except the teetotal Beatie had a tumbler of it, yellowish and winking; even I had a wine glass full, presumably to bring me up in the right way. Joan and Bill had fizzy lemonade. The pudding was spotted dog, with thick cold custard, which I specially liked with a hot pudding, and a plentiful sprinkling of a brown sugar, soft and agglomerated, called 'pieces', as I was surprised to learn. We got the giggles spelling G U T T Z Z Z in deaf-and-dumb language on our fingers to one another at the small table, as a comment on everyone's appetite, including ours, the three Zs prodded out with the right hand tapped against the left elbow. Then they drank tea, and we children were released to tread very softly in the garden until undertaker Ben had finished his share of the chores, when we went, well wrapped up, with him and his lazy dog to the local park and worked off our intake.

But soon it was time to go back to Inverness Terrace as we couldn't possibly be accommodated in this doll's house, and there were tearful farewells and kisses all round, and promises of early reunions and wavings at the front door till we turned the corner. As we waited for our bus it began to spit with rain. At the time I don't believe I noticed the wild contrast in social class between Dulwich and Bayswater: in those days they were merely different but equally astonishing. I saw variation but no implications in the spaciousness of Inverness Terrace after the cramped little house in Dulwich, the way you didn't have to crouch and swerve to get a book or pass a plate, and you found that there were some empty chairs even after the assembly had gathered.

During this trip Florence took the three of us to the Natural History Museum at South Kensington. I had a quick look at the bird gallery, but the other three were more interested in the reconstructed skeletons of Diplodocus and other primeval creatures. We all gasped at the Giant Squid which was suspended above our heads and seemed thirty or forty feet long. Then they went off to look at stuffed mammals while I spent some time alone gloating over the collection of English Butterflies. The rows of uniformly perfect insects in those smoothly running glass-topped mahogany drawers made me green with envy but also made me determined to emulate them. I dreamed of twenty or even sixty-drawer cabinets where I could lay the whole collection out with no sense of confinement. I saw that these drawers full of peerless beauties were arranged in the same way as Kirby's book – in their Natural Orders – and decided that I would do the same.

I returned to Owslebury determined to scrap my poor specimens, rearrange my whole collection, and start again, leaving spaces for the ones I would soon catch or somehow acquire. Like the South Ken. collection mine must have several of each species – at least two of the male upperside and underside, and the same for the female – a minimum of eight specimens for each variety. I helped my father to line cigar boxes with strip cork, and he fitted two of them with glass tops cut with a borrowed glass cutter; but it is extraordinary how much space a few dead insects need, and I was aware of a conflict between the available space and the butterflies I actually had. Mr Last, whom I felt I knew very well by now, and who warmly approved of my devotion to the butterfly world, gave me a discarded case of his own, which had a cork lined base and lid; the white paper was badly stained and blotted, but my father, neat-fingered as always, relined it meticulously. I was very proud of this case, with its brass hooks and eyes, but there was only one. I was a bit mystified by the way Mr Last could have up to thirty butterflies pinned in the lid part and another thirty in the case itself without the pins ever fouling one another.

In this one really good box I planned to start with the *Pieridae*, that is the Whites and Yellows, as all good entomologists should. So I began measuring, bearing in mind that I must have eight butterflies, or gaps, for each species. I started at the top left-hand corner allotting places for my eight Large Cabbage Whites, followed by my eight Small Cabbage Whites, my five Green-Veined Whites with spaces for three, and then my one ragged specimen of the Wood White, followed by seven spaces. Next in the butterfly book came the Black-Veined White, which had been caught only about ten times in England in the last thirty years, but for consistency this must be given eight spaces. Then would come the Brimstones of which I had three – two good males and a tatty female – with spaces for five . . . there was just room in the case for eight gaps for the Pale Clouded Yellow. My best case was full – or rather half empty – and I had covered eight out of the total of sixty-four British species, and what's more I'd forgotten the Orange Tip completely. It was impossible.

Even after the butterflies and the bigger moths, which I

had started on in a cigar box, there were the *Microlepidoptera*, containing tiny moths in thousands of species, though mercifully the undersides were all pretty much the same. Then, the already enormous landscape stretching to infinity, I was given by a parent of one of my schoolmates a box of foreign butterflies, some from France and Belgium, and a lot from Ceylon and India. Vast territories, the map of the whole world swarming with butterflies, excited and yet depressed me. And then, as if that were not enough, I had some beetles, some dragonflies, and a few flies and wasps and bees caught dispiritedly last autumn in a longing to use my net after 'the season' was over. Could I collect all these as well, even if I wanted to? It was fantastic; it was wonderful; it was utterly depressing.

In this kind of confusion I spent hours and hours in the tiny chilly pantry; setting, hunting things up in books and hoping I wasn't kidding myself about the rarer ones; rearranging on a brand-new scheme, borrowing my father's Indian ink and his sharp penknife and preparing elaborate sets of labels which occupied far too much space. Live butterflies are fragile, light and short-lived enough, but dead in a cabinet, especially a home-made one, their life is short indeed. While my commonplace Cabbage Whites and Meadow Browns always stood up unharmed to the attack of any number of mites, the rarer ones seemed more vulnerable, and now that the butterfly 'season' was coming round again, some of the best specimens were represented by a little blob or pile of grey tindery stuff (I believe called 'frass') or a little dribble of grease, with a pair of forlorn wings still floating in the air on the pin. The camphor ball I always put hopefully in the corner, which was supposed to destroy mites, seemed ineffective, and once it rolled out of its supporting palisade of pins and banged around the box smashing everything in its way. In spite of such frustrations, I went to bed night after night dazzled and enraptured, in a cloud of wings and pins and Latin names.

Leslie Binder, who remained an acquaintance rather than a close friend, and who was so strikingly different in vocabulary and manner from most of my classmates, was an only child. One thing about the Binders surprised me a bit, as they seemed to have plenty of money to buy all the food they needed: they spent a lot of time collecting and preserving everything wild and edible at the due seasons – fungi, fruit, flowers for wine-making. All their expeditions seemed to be concerned with harvesting, nutting, or collecting herbs – a risky procedure most of the village thought, with all those poisonous plants around the place. But the beautiful young widowed Mrs Binder was utterly confident and casual about such risks, assuring us that the little yellow toadstools in her basket were chanterelles – 'Unmistakable,' she said. 'They smell of apricots.' On the infrequent occasions when we met Leslie he was always with his mother.

So it was a surprise when one Friday afternoon at school in late April, Leslie told me he would be passing our cottage next morning on the way to collect cowslips to make wine, and invited me to go with him. He walked all the way from Baybridge with a very large dark-wicker basket, and knocked at our front door, looking cool and immaculate as usual. Bill decided he'd like to come too, so Florence gave us her own shopping basket and we set off, aiming at a promising area his mother had suggested. This was somewhere a good way beyond the track behind the Southgate's cottage, along a wooded lane which unaccountably turned later into a proper surfaced road. The morning was milky and lush, and we walked along through the green shade dappled occasionally with discs of sunlight. Bill and I chewed some of the triangular beech-nuts which still lay thickly under the trees, and though I suggested after trying a couple that they were long past their best, Bill went on eating them. I didn't think it mattered as there was an inordinate amount of opening and chewing for a very small reward in the way of kernel, so I could hardly be blamed for allowing him to 'spoil his dinner'; a mouthful of actual nut would take an hour or so to accumulate.

At length we came out from the tunnel of trees into bright spring sunlight, and began looking for cowslips. The pasture fields seemed blankly green except for daisies, dandelions and buttercups, and the steep hedgerow banks were patched only with dying primroses and yellow deadnettle, which Bill for a moment mistook for cowslips, as being at least the right colour. A labourer who worked for Farmer Gale clumped up the road on a bareback horse carrying a flowering stick of wild cherry instead of a whip, and as we shrank into the hedgeside from his slow-moving conker-coloured horse, slightly unnerved by its large ringing feet, he greeted us from his surprising height.

'Where you goin' to?' he asked.

'Looking for cowslips.'

'Plenty up the road, mebbe half a mile, on the old leas. Can't missum.'

Half a mile was a bit daunting, but the news was encouraging, and Leslie, who was well brought up and always polite in a way I found faintly enviable, said 'Thank you very much' and 'Is there a bull?' (knowing why cowslips are so called).

'No, only a few owd cows – they won't bother you. They 'udn't hurt a fly' – this over his shoulder as he rode slowly on. It seemed to me that he was in a good position to know the location of cows and cowslips and indeed of bulls, as he could see right over the hedges.

So we kept our eyes skinned, and on a turn in the road saw suddenly a patch of pale colour, high up on the hedge bank and hard to get at. Then I remembered that you find cowslips not by seeing the beautiful pale yellow, which is not conspicuous, especially in the confused herbage of a hedgerow, and even less by the fascinating orange spots and the peppery delicate smell. No, you first saw the creamy pale green of the calyces and the stems, and this is what the patch was when we scrambled up to get them, the flowers hanging dimly and hardly open. Soon we spotted another little patch down near the edge of the road, and then, as the road curved and dipped again, a whole field in which there were scattered patches of the same colour – more and more, it seemed, as we climbed the bank. We yanked Bill after us, scratched our bare legs on the autumn-cut hawthorns, and I lifted the barbed wire with coat-protected fingers and a boot on the lower strand while Leslie got through neatly and Bill rather untidily – catching his socks, trousers and even his hair. We looked towards the dozen cows and they looked up at us, but they didn't seem very interested and were soon back munching the rich spring grass. So we picked, first every fat stem rising neatly from the starfish leaves spreadeagled in the grass, and soon, getting harder to please, I collected only the longest-stemmed flowers, while Leslie doggedly went on gathering anything showing colour.

Bill dashed from patch to patch shouting 'Look, these are e*nor*mous!' causing the cows to look up again. Bill tended, as I mildly complained, to pick the long stems about half-way down; these would be fine for wine and should have gone into Leslie's basket, but Bill insisted on putting them into ours, where they rather spoiled the look of the bunch. However, he was often distracted, by hover-flies and beetles and a jay suddenly squawking nearby. We picked a good bunch for my mother and wrapped them in long juicy grasses twined round the stems. As I moved from patch to patch through the grass-scented air I could see the tender differences of spring colour in the hedgerow of trees dividing the fields down the slope.

We skirted the cows which were cropping the lushest grasses in the valley, and came to a patch of hazel coppice. After a moment I recognised it as a wood we had visited more than once with Florence and Arthur, but always from the valley road below and never from this direction. To my surprise the tall hazel trees had all gone, and there were still wood chips lying about and white steppings on the tree stumps to show that the cutting had been recent. What I remembered was catkins dangling in February, and in September neatly cloaked hazel-nuts accessible only to my father's curved walking-stick handle; but now the area was open to the skies, and the sunlight hit the long-hidden patches of rich growth. There were still cushions of moss spiked with tiny pink clubs, and what remained of a rich woodland flora, the sunlight helping some and beginning to bleach others. The wood anemones, fine-cut leaves and poised flowers stained with purple, looked a bit surprised; they were, as I knew, sadly useless for picking and in any case nearly over. What dominated the bumpy mossy slope, however, were oxlips, their flowers half-way between the pale tragic beauty of the fading primroses and the richer splendour of the cowslips; I had never seen them before in such quantity. Twice the size of cowslips, they had large bunches of hanging flowers on stout stems, the petals close in colour to the calyces, so the general effect was of a carpet of acid cream – a contradiction in terms which I can't resolve.

Anyway, we thought they were lovely, and while Leslie went on steadily picking the few cowslips there were on the edge of the coppice, Bill and I gathered a big bunch and a few leaves to go with them. Interplanted, as it were, between the large patches of oxlips were smaller areas of violets, the dog violet and the purple-scented one, ground ivy and cuckoo pint. The general effect was tessellated like a pavement or juxtaposed like a patchwork, all contrasting with the grey bark and white heartwood of the hazel stumps, and all surprisingly glowing in the open air instead of hidden in the early shade and leafiness of the wood. Later Frankie Southgate told me that the wood, called Jessy's Copse, was coppiced every twelve years, and he had helped to cut this one; indeed, some of the sacks of brushwood he regularly provided for Florence had come from this very coppice, and that thought for some reason pleased me very much.

A bit further down the slope we came to a completely different scene – a dampish tussocky field, scarred by old pitted cowpats; here there were big patches of ladies' smocks and kingcups, and smaller drifts of early purple orchids. They were juicy and their stems squeaked a bit as I gathered them and bunched them together, leaving the speckled leaves in their pairs, and taking only the flowering heads with their strange, sickly, exciting smell. A bunch of a dozen seemed a rich present, and I pictured jam jars all along the window sills in the cottage sitting-room.

We had some broken biscuits with us, and these we shared meticulously in the spring sunlight, pleased with the contents of our baskets. Leslie's was heaped with cowslips but in ours were neatly grouped bunches – oxlips, cowslips, a few violets, and the vivid cornerpiece of purple orchids. We wandered and dawdled back up the slope, under and over and between the barbed wire, up the hot road and along the lane, Bill and I bumping the basket with increasing groans – it was a bit big for us and wrongly shaped to share. We were tired by now, and relieved to put the basket down while I plunged into a thicket of lightly leaved hawthorn, where I could see two nests. One I sadly reported to Bill as 'last year's', the other, more cheerfully, as 'Building – might be a bullfinch'. Bill meanwhile scuffed in last year's leaves and tried a few more beech-nuts. Just beyond was a small stand of larches, which meant we were nearly home; they showed early puffs of startling green leaf with pink blossom.

At last we came out on to the corner and went up the little slope to the Shearers, where Leslie settled down to wait to be picked up by a van delivering cowcake to Baybridge and driven by a friend of his family. We hoped his cowslips wouldn't be too wilted but apparently it didn't matter for wine – and ours were soon on display, with tiny bubbles of water clinging to the fat stems of the oxlips. They looked a bit dumpy, as all my arrangements tended to, but smelt interesting and brightened the place up. I put a small pot in My Museum on the rough table which always seemed a bit gritty, but though they smelt good as I looked up 'Oxlips' in *Flowers of the Field*, they didn't last long in the dark little room, and by tea-time were curved despondently all round the edge of the pot, the flower-heads touching the grit, their elegant three-dimensionality flattened out. Still, the ones in the sitting-room survived for a couple of days, and were admired by my father when he got back that evening from a day out 'on business' with the Ansteys.

PART FIVE

Paradise Gained and Lost

CHAPTER THIRTEEN

MORE NESTS AND MORE PEOPLE

One day I was on the flinty footpath half-way to Baybridge, waiting for Bobby Botwright more impatiently than usual, because in the middle of the thick overgrown blackthorn to my left I could see quite clearly a green grasshopper totally immobile and at a very strange angle, and beyond it, impossibly blurred by the proliferating branches, stems, twigs, thorns and puffs of green, a dark mass that might – could it possibly be? My heart went faster. I knew that the red-backed shrike kept a larder on a thorn tree; and my bird book showed a bumble-bee and a beetle impaled on a thorn by its nest, and that was why it was called a butcher-bird. But the nest looked quite inaccessible, though with Bobby's help I might possibly reach it. And it was the right time of year – late in May and already very hot outside the shade of the thorn hedge. I stood quite still and hoped for the bird to appear but there was no sign and no sound – except, as I gradually realised, for the larks in the sky and the partridges over in the field, and the lapwings circling and even the birds in the Baybridge rookery cawing faintly in the sunny distance. Then Bobby did appear, running like a small cart-horse, all boots and long serge shorts, his socks down round his boots as they always were.

'Sorry I'm late, Pete. Me mum told me to get her in some taters and then I had to feed me rabbits, and I gotta be back for dinner.' I brushed his apologies aside and we struggled to get into the middle of the thorn bush. We soon saw that it was indeed a nest, large, untidy, and made, it seemed, of dried clumps of grass, as if the bird had pulled these up by the roots. After many attempts Bobby lent me his jacket to put over my jersey, as I was supposed to be the expert. The navy-blue serge felt strange on my wrists and it smelt of paraffin and onions and frying pans, but it was very welcome to protect my arms and front. Meanwhile Bobby leant against part of the bush with my haversack to protect his thin-shirted back from the vicious thorns. The nest was not very well hidden, but well protected and hardly reachable from an angle. There was a dead cockchafer skewered on an adjoining thorn and in the last struggles my face was close enough to it for me to see its surprised expression. Somehow, on tiptoe, I got my hand up and over the rim of the nest. It was warm but empty. Still, it must have a resident with all that larder; so we tried to restore some order into the rather bashed-up looking bush, and even tidied up our footprints in the long grass, in the hope that she wouldn't desert. Our scratched arms and hands stung a little.

Ten days later I walked back again after school with Bobby, on his way home, as far as the hedge. We hadn't told a soul and believed the nest was a secret of ours. As we started on the outer defences a silent bird came off the nest and vanished. We got through the palisades of thorns somehow, more quickly and easily than before. The larder had gone, which made me wonder if there were young already – but no, the nest, still warm, had three eggs, and on tiptoe I could just get my fingers round one and take it gently out: a beautiful egg, surprisingly large, I thought, a pale pinkish brown like beechwood, marked with gorgeous brown spots gathered into a zone at the fat end. The struggle to get out of the bush endangered the lovely egg, so I put it in my mouth for protection, and we could only exchange congratulations when we were back on the path and I had taken it out and shown it to Bobby. We put it tenderly in my empty lunch box lined with grass we had pulled from the hedge bottom, and I hurried home so as not to be late for supper. I arrived just in time for rabbit stew, so I had to wait to blow my shrike's egg. I thought it better than any Great Northern Diver and was proud of this rather uncommon egg which I had actually found myself.

Two other nests, among the dozens I found that season, remain in my memory – one shared with the whole family, the other never seen except by me. I was helping Bill to sow his favourite radishes one bright May morning – the kind of morning when we could smell the goosegrass as it scrambled up the bushes with the speed of Jack's beanstalk, and the wild garlic which had colonised every undug square foot along the hedge bottom. We were on Bill's patch in the acute angle at the far end of the garden, and beyond us was a boundary fence overgrown with shrubs but still visible, made of a rusty bedstead with one tarnished and peeling brass knob, a couple of angle irons, and some bits of iron piping about three feet out of the ground. We pulled out the weeds in the hot soil, raked them into the hedge and, with a stick, drew two short rather unsteady drills.

Then I went up to the barn to get the old galvanised watering-can to fill it from the well – to soak the two drills. I struggled a bit down the path, bent like Atlas with the weight. Bill signalled to me to come quietly; he looked a bit excited, and I wondered whether it was yet another Peacock butterfly sunning itself with flat wings on a stone. I shared his feeling that they were lovely, but considered them entomologically boring because they were so common. There was more elaborate miming from Bill. When I reached him and put the heavy can down he thought it appropriate to whisper, so quietly that I couldn't hear, so I said, 'What?' loudly enough for him to shush me before he repeated the message. I was close to giggles before I gathered that he had seen a little bird with a dark head going into the metal pipe in the hedge and it was in there now. From his height he had a good view through the intervening greenery, and I knelt to watch with him, expecting a bird to emerge, but in fact one startlingly arrived instead, a grey and white bird with a blackish head, carrying quite a long trail of dried grass. It landed on the metal rim for a moment, and vanished into the pipe. I was pleased with Bill and his naturalist's eye – I had never looked down the hole of this bit of piping or thought of it as a nesting site. I gave him a little hug when I said, 'I think it's a blackcap, and it must be building a nest down there.'

We went straight up to the house and consulted the Landsborough Thompson book. The plate came nearly at the end but we didn't have the wit to use the index, and were sidetracked by many of the earlier pictures. At last we reached the blackcap, the male bird shown with a glossy black patch on his head, sitting complacently with his beak open on an apple-tree branch in full blossom. It was the right season we knew, as our apples were in bloom, and the bird looked right. By the time we got back to the radish patch the drills were bone dry and we shared the job of slopping the already lukewarm water into them, making them smell delicious but look a bit puddly. As we sowed the round radish seed, probably rather too thickly – Bill from one end and I from the other – the male blackcap arrived twice. Once he dropped a length of moss when he was perched again on the metal edge and was suddenly moved to produce a short flourish of soft and melodious song. We told Florence when she got back with Joan, and we were all forbidden to disturb the birds by going too close or watching too often, though they seemed completely fearless and indifferent to my presence.

It was perhaps a fortnight later that I, who had of course been taking surreptitious looks down the hole while the bird was off, first saw the nest, a little way down, silkily finished off, and lined with horsehair; and then the steady appearance of eggs, one a day, for five days. This involved also seeing the bird 'on', its neck forced upwards, I thought, by the unyielding metal as much as the nest-rim. It looked a bit anguished, though all the sitting birds I had seen had the same indignant hard-eyed stare. I hadn't got a blackcap's egg, though I had seen them and had been told that they were hard to distinguish from the garden warbler's, and down in the pipe it was too shadowy to be sure of the exact colour or markings. I was determined to have one, but my parents, though they knew perfectly well that I collected eggs, felt a proprietary interest in this particular nest. I felt sure they greatly exaggerated the vulnerability of birds to an occasional gentle inspection; in fact I thought the birds rather liked me. So I waited till my mother and sister were over at the Shearers talking to the Chenerys, before I quietly approached the post. No bird was 'on' and the metal was warm in the sun; down inside was the little cradle with five tiny eggs. I put my hand in but it wouldn't go; even my small wrist and knuckles met resistance and there was no hope of getting that far down. So I decided to take Bill into my confidence, especially as it was his post; he was its first finder, and, like Cook Island in the atlas, it should, I thought, be called Bill's Post. As he was too short to reach up and then have enough arm to spare for reaching down, I lifted him, but there was a bit too much muscular strain, making us both red with exertion, and Bill perhaps also with anxiety. So we propped him up by standing him on the end of a wooden box from the barn; I held his shoulders, and we both held our breath. His hand went in fairly easily and I told him to take one egg, get it into the palm of his hand, and then slowly withdraw his arm. He did this shakily, gasping a bit, but entirely successfully, and handed the exquisite little object triumphantly to me. It was greenish olive, densely blotched with a darker olivish green, and he let me carry it up to the house and blow it and put it safely in the collection while, stumblingly and with frequent stops for breath, he humped the big box back to the barn by himself.

When Florence and Joan got back our secret was complete and all evidence destroyed. Next day, thank heavens, the two birds were cheerfully going back and forth, up and down to the nest. Then, one Saturday morning, Bill and I heard a series of high-pitched squeaks from the tube, and my parents delightedly allowed themselves to be shown the four gaping babies with their diamond-shaped pale-pink mouths wide open, their pathetic naked bodies occasionally visible. It seemed quite safe to show any visitors this rare sight, and the two parent birds went on unconcernedly bringing large beakfuls of leggy insects to their insatiable brood. Gradually the nestlings turned into four rather squashed-looking fast-breathing feathered lumps, and then one day they were not there, and there was only the empty dry nest with a pale fragment or two of eggshell. Meanwhile my own whole shell was safely housed alongside the whitethroat and the garden warbler – in my view the three Graces – different, yet the same. Later in the year Bill and I stuffed newspaper in the top of the tube to keep the rain out, hoping that the blackcaps would come again next spring.

That same spring I was nest-hunting on my own up a hot little lane hedged on one side and banked on the other, too narrow for anything but a small cart. It led to Morestead Warren farm, and wound casually up between rough and rising fields and out on to a patch of heathland with a solitary tin barn on the skyline. Hardly anyone ever seemed to use the lane, and to me it was a treasury of bird and insect life. I was hunting among the lush growth of hedgerow flowers, and found the beginnings of a nest in dried grass at the end of what might have been a grass tunnel, though it was not very clear or determinate. I knew this was the trademark of a chiffchaff, and looked forward to the prospect of seeing my first chiffchaff's nest. I registered the exact spot – on the opposite side of the road to a large patch of a plant called houndstongue, with silky brown blossom and smelling strongly of mice, or rather of a large and unventilated mouse's nest. I was just moving on up the lane when my eye caught a patch of vivid colour in the hedge above. Placed with consummate neatness in the elbow of a hawthorn branch was a nest lined with white wool and containing three sky-blue eggs; only a hedge sparrow, and like the peacock butterfly, beautiful, but not exciting.

After the statutory wait for developments which features in all these birds nesting stories I went back with some anticipation one evening after school. The chiffchaff's nest, if that is what it was, hadn't developed at all, and I was disappointed that my diagnosis had been wrong, or perhaps I had caused the bird to desert. Dispiritedly I pulled aside the hawthorn twigs above the site, and there was a sudden lurch of excitement and surprise. In the little off-white cup there were four sky-blue eggs and one larger rounder dark-grey-and-spotted egg! My first cuckoo's egg, with none of the possible doubt about identification there might be in a meadow pipit's nest, in which the cuckoo's egg looks more or less the same as those of the rightful owners. I took it and put it carefully in the cotton-wool lined box, feeling for once a total absence of guilt and rapacity, but instead a conviction that I was doing active good for the mother hedge sparrow. She was now fluttering and cheeping loudly in the next bush, and I felt I was saving her from having her fledglings elbowed out of the nest to die on the ground below, while she broke her back feeding the gross and greedy interloper – a story I had so often read and which seemed so unfair.

Thus for once cupidity and benefit to birds coincided, and the few experts who saw my collection and questioned the identification of the not very distinctly marked egg were told the story in meticulous detail – the chiffchaff's tunnel, the houndstongue, the wool lining, the three eggs, the return, the surprise, the alarmed hen-bird – till I even bored myself by the repetition, and Bill and Joan studied the visitor's face rather more than mine, to see if the narrative had lost its original excitement.

Florence and Arthur had long been on at least nodding terms with the Havertons, but as a family it was only now that we got to know them. This was mainly, I suspect, because they weren't overkeen about young children in their elegant house – a smallish grey house between us and the Pooleys, decorated with yellow climbing roses, backed by trees and with a properly designed garden. Yet their bit of the road was always splashed or dotted with cowpats, and when you walked up their long front path the pong from the farmyard over the parallel wall reminded you of what their wealth was based on. When Joan, Bill and I played in the barn the game called 'Gwen, Charles and Gerald', we acted out our fantasies of taxis and restaurants and all the indications of wealth and glamour, and it was on the Havertons that we modelled ourselves. I don't think they ever came into the cottage, so we met on neutral ground – the cricket field, the village hall, occasional functions at school; once or twice we were invited to tea at the house. As our cottage belonged to the Havertons I thought it was rather nice of them to be so matey.

Mr Haverton was so thin that he went in where most people went out, and was built rather like a marabou stork, his very small bald head always topped by a tweed hat. I was impressed by his jacket being leather-bound on both arms from cuff to elbow, something I had never seen before. He wore superior boots and well-polished gaiters. I was told that he had been decorated for gallantry in the war when he served with a yeomanry regiment. Certainly he had the right sort of bearing, but his eyes seemed indeterminately blue and vague for the dogged character I pictured as hero from short stories in *London Opinion* and *Nash's Magazine* about such goings-on. He shaved close and neat apart from a Charlie Chan moustache, but he left a couple of owl-patches like Frankie Southgate's on the upper part of each cheek which linked in a curve with the hair above his ears. He was a veiny man: a prominent vein the colour of his skimmed-milk eyes showed on his temples and complex deltas of thick veins covered the backs of his hands. He walked briskly and yet with a langorous upper-class insolence which we spotted and even tried to imitate. He often carried a springy little whip or cane, and when he wanted my father he would rat-a-tat sharply on the cottage door with this; it gave him a briskness at odds with the pale eyes and quiet voice.

Mr Haverton probably provided my first local glimpse of class and class divisions, complicated in my view by our own ambiguous status as a family which talked posh but often hadn't got two ha'pennies to rub together. His remoteness and superiority to the rest of us in Owslebury Bottom was neatly symbolised by his being so often on horseback, and looking down on us in every sense from a great height. His horse was dark brown and close-clipped – a lively, hoof-ringing and slightly menacing animal; and the Haverton leggings and spotless boots, a few inches above my nose, had clearly never been near a farmyard. He used his short whip not only for rapping at our door but also for saluting my mother by holding it upright alongside his tweed cap, his other hand for a moment grasping a large handful of rein and thus causing the horse to rear alarmingly. I once heard Frankie Southgate say to Florence 'That Colonel Averton e's allus poloite and noice to me an me family, but he int loiked not by themas works for im. Oi don' loike im meself, no I don't.'

Mrs Haverton was white-haired, tweeded like her husband when she wasn't wearing her pearls, and had a faded English rose expression and complexion. Miniatures and silhouettes decorated her walls and she had roses in rosebowls. When we went to tea, she served a superior Dundee cake, the slices edged with faintly browned almonds, and simultaneously damp and crumbly. We sat on the edge of her cretonned armchairs while tea was served – china tea with lemon, which I thought very odd, tasting of tar, and not at all like real tea. As the cake slices were handed round I was conscious of the beautiful lines of her small Georgian window looking out on a whole row of flowering lavenders, and the general elegance of the surroundings. There were rugs dotted about the dark polished floorboards; close-piled, they made a contrast with our friendlier crackly goatskins and our red carpet strip. I became very aware of the size and cragginess of my boots resting on these impressive rectangles, and hoped they wouldn't seem conspicuously huge or too obviously home-repaired. Below the bow window stood the famous chaise-longue, looking oddly assymmetrical. Its back curved down to nothing, its headprop ended in a fat cylinder set off with a wooden spiral, and it was upholstered in the palest creamy-green silk; the accompanying sausage-shaped cushion was striped in this pale green and a toning pale cream. The whole thing was beautiful but a bit daunting. Even if the Havertons didn't use it for sitting – and they didn't – I felt it would make an even more unsuitable resting place for my own buttocks than the thick creamy rugs did for my thick craggy boots.

There were no sons, but two or three plumpish high-coloured grown-up daughters, not married but hoping to be, and in the meantime busying themselves with good works in the village – Women's Institute meetings with Dot Pooley and the distaff Hunneys, and playing games with the likes of us. One day a handful of children were playing on the field behind the Havertons' house, and these well-spoken well-rounded ladies were organising us. They wore cashmere sweaters which stressed their convexities, and tweed skirts with decorous checks: up close they smelt scrubbed. The game involved one of us being in the middle surrounded by the rest, and I was wearing a new shirt blouse made of shantung which my mother had just finished and which I secretly thought looked a bit strange on me. As they were chanting the rhymes of the game, one rounded lady said to another in ringing, ruling-class tones, 'Doesn't Peter look common?' It didn't seem to me a very strange or inappropriate remark to make – I wasn't conscious of all the nuances of the term, but when I repeated it to my mother on my return to the cottage the response was surprising and instantaneous. She went scarlet with indignation and dashed upstairs to smother herself in powder and cram on her cloche hat, to walk down the road and 'have it out with them'. Mercifully this never happened because as she was actually leaving the house, Joan arrived home and assured her that I'd got it wrong, and what they had actually said was 'Doesn't Peter look *solemn*?' Embarrassed Florence, pinker than ever, laughing and ashamed, drew back from the brink, and the story was repeated with delight for some years.

The only other thing I remember about the Havertons is that they had a dozen or so guinea-fowl which ran with the hens but, like their furniture, these creatures were fascinatingly different. They were pear-shaped, almost legless, with beautiful spotted feathers that exactly echoed the hen-like but spotted eggs they laid – and we collected both eggs and feathers. One or two of the daughters had already moved away and wedding photographs in oval silver frames sat behind the rosebowl on the shaky little mahogany table. There seemed to be undertones of sadness in Mrs Haverton's sitting-room in spite of the tarry tea and the damp cake slices and the furniture polish and all the splendour surrounding us, as if somehow opportunities had been missed and would never come again. So though she was always thoughtful and nice to us, I was not displeased to walk back down the road to the wood-smoke and paraffin smell of the cottage.

I can't think of a stronger social contrast at that time of my life than the Havertons, in their sitting-room, and Ernie Bone, in a ditch. He and Mr Haverton were both war veterans.

Ernie seemed determined to frighten small children. Once he cornered a group of us, after school, long enough to describe in half-intelligible words but loving detail how he had trapped, killed and eaten a badger, and, inconsequentially, but in a way riveting to his audience, just how old Mrs Thatcher had gouged her eye out falling off a ladder. As far as the village children were concerned his knife was a murder weapon, and stories of unsolved deaths in neighbouring villages like Chilcomb and Upham were always and inevitably blamed on him. More than once I had to pass this figure on the road, a gross and yet thin bundle hung about with little bags and sacks, and I always searched urgently for a footpath, a garden, a gate I could slip through to avoid the encounter.

Once I saw him sitting on a flat bit of ditch beyond the Shearers hidden by surrounding bushes as if he were in a little leafy room. His possessions lay round him, a heap of grisly-looking clothing on one sack, and a variety of enamel vessels propped uneasily on the spring grass. He sat on another sack, and he was frying half a dozen bright-yoked eggs over a little pile of burning twigs in a horrible saucepan which I recognised as I had seen it hanging from his back. This time he surprised and alarmed me by being for once almost amiable, and said they were blackbirds' eggs. He added, 'Magpies' is lovely, but you ave to climb. Peewits' is best but they're buggers to find in the plough.' He boasted of catching hedgehogs and even mice, but I declined his invitation to sit with him on the excuse of a pressing errand, as I watched him slice a hunk of bread with his alarmingly familiar knife. 'Frightened of tramps, are yer?' he shouted after me as I hurried down the road.

Ernie often slept in the open – in a ditch, on beech leaves under some sheltering trees, in the lee of a cowbyre. He looked when prone like a pile of old sacks, but on being disturbed or merely hearing voices, he would leap up suddenly and hurl oaths and curses at us for disturbing his sleep, even though it was already mid-morning. He brandished an open clasp-knife. It was the only bright thing about him, his eyes being dulled and his teeth yellow and blurred with slime, and this bright narrow-tipped blade held upright in his fist symbolised his power. Whenever there were minor mishaps in the area – cattle food or chicken meal missing, a pig found dead, washing gone from the line – people felt that it wasn't an accident, carelessness or petty theft by children; no, it was Ernie Bone. The feeling he inspired in the village kids was uniform: even the toughest of my school-fellows was unwilling to joke about Ernie Bone. Two sentences were certain to clutch and squeeze the small hearts of all of us in Owslebury Bottom; one was 'The bull's loose!' – Havertons' bull being the epitome of danger, though as far as I know it had never hurt a fly; the other, said in a whisper with round and frightened eyes, was 'Ernie Bone's here again! Gerry White saw him going up Jackman's Hill, Mr Hyden said he was in Morestead this morning and walking this way.' He was like a plague or blight on our lives.

For some years Ernie came into my dreams; nightmares in which he slowly emerged from the yellow mist or driving snow and was finally revealed in close-up, with his bloodshot eyes the colour of his trade, spittle and rheum at the corners of eyes and beard, and his bright blade held up at an angle to pierce my constricted and terrified heart. I would hear his wicked words which he bellowed or, even worse, whispered at me. He was at the opposite end of the spectrum of my life from the Orange-Tips, Underwings and Sally's mocking flickering touch on my sleeve. He embodied something hopeless and hideous in contrast with beauty and excitement.

CHAPTER FOURTEEN

LOVE, LUST, LEPIDOPTERA

Before school in the morning I sometimes prowled around the Medder, and if there was no better game, I might catch another of the brown butterflies called for some strange reason Gatekeepers. I rather despised them as they were so common, but one of my underside specimens had a feeler mising. I was always replacing the more available butterflies, only to find that I had filled up my setting boards and then got something really worth having and had to set it on a piece of naked wood. My new net could be dismantled, and during the really hot days I could take it to school, the ring and muslin in my satchel, and the handle used as a walking-stick. More than once I was late because I had seen something worth catching, and Joan and Bill would follow it, jumping and stumbling over tussocky grass on the hillside, while I tried breathlessly to assemble the net. A commoner way was to use my school cap, hurling myself on to the settled butterfly, and then with infinite care rolling the cap back inch by inch until a bit of wing or a few waving legs showed. Often this comedy was played while the school bell finished ringing three fields away and Joan leapt up and down in agony, and I found that the cap contained nothing but grass.

The first spring day was for me, in the butterfly world, not the day when an odd Cabbage White appeared or a tired Small Tortoiseshell, faded and dishevelled, blundered into the warm sun from its hibernation in the barn rafters, but the day of the first Orange Tip. I would be well into the birdsnesting season and perhaps looking for a yellowhammer's nest in the long grass on the sunny side of the hedge, and a male Orange Tip butterfly would flutter on to a doily-shaped head of hedge parsley nearby. Instantly the nest would be forgotten and I would stare entranced at the newness and richness of it, a freshness which was as completely familiar as the smell of one's own house after a long absence. The apex of both forewings is a bright rich orange, an odd and lovely colour in that season of whites and pale pinks; but what gave it character for me was the underneath of the hind wing, which was a mottled soft green on a white ground, the green exactly of the fluted hedge-parsley stems over which it hovered. The yellowhammer's nest might not be there, and even if it was I might trample on it by accident, but this Orange Tip, this *Euchloe cardamines*, this glorious common thing was there for the taking – or would be if I had my net, and my collecting box, and my pins, and my setting boards . . . That was the evening when I got out my butterfly books and looked at my collection and dusted the glass. And I remembered that the female Orange Tip had no orange, but only black tips, so that it could be confused on the wing with the common Green-Veined White, but that the underside was also this mottled soft green, and it seemed absolutely right that it should be so.

Later in the season I could sometimes give a whole day more or less exclusively to catching butterflies. My mother was usually up at about seven; she woke me on school days, but in 'the season' I was often up first. If it was a weekend my father – who generally arrived late on Friday evening – was always the first to come downstairs and would boil a kettle on sticks in the grate or on a primus stove, and wander matily along the garden path with me, telling me that 'your Mother' was tired, or arranging some special treat for her. Once or twice he asked whether I should be able to get to the cricket match that afternoon as they might be short of someone to score. I hedged politely, but in the height of the butterfly season managed to be a long way off until tea-time at least. After breakfast I got my butterfly kit ready. I also took jam sandwiches, an apple or a slice of cake, and a flat bottle with a cork (the glass embossed with Woodwards Cough Linctus) for drinking-water, which got lukewarm long before lunch. My father's old army haversack took it all.

On one such day I walked up the Bottom road in the warming sun and tried not to be led aside by any attractions in the adjoining fields but pushed on up Crabbe's Hill in the deep shade of the beeches, then out again on Cobb's Corner and finally through a tiny path between flint walls and on to the open field-path to Baybridge. Bobby Botwright, as usual rather silent, met me at the point where the hard flinty path passed through a diagonal thorn hedge – the exact spot where we found the nest of the butcher-bird, the red-backed shrike. We moved off along the shady side of the hedge, still wet with dew, catching our long socks on vagrant thongs of bramble, seeing the yellow and blush buds of the honeysuckle about us and the faint ephemeral flowers of the dogrose everywhere. Blues and Small Heaths and Coppers rested or flirted their wings on the hardheads and hogweed in the patches of sunlight which broke through the old hedge, but we stuck to our path: we were out for bigger, or at least rarer, game. Soon we got to Longwood Spinney, a grove of downy birch and alder and blackthorn on bumpy ground, petering out vaguely at intervals into dry heathland and then appearing again in a hollow or on the flank of a hill.

At one prized point the trees gave way to a patch of marshy land, rare in our immediate area and therefore highly valued, where fleabane and watermint grew. Here we always expected to catch a Swallow-Tail, dramatically yellow and black with tails on the lower wings, though every book I had seen said firmly that they were to be found only in the extensive fens of Cambridgeshire. I knew they needed large patches of water, but it seemed such a perfect spot for them – a marsh perhaps fifty yards across, surrounded by dry uplands. I could almost see the superb insect floating across the water-iris, and resting for a minute with quivering wings on a purple flower growing from an old hoof-mark among the tough grasses and the darting dragonflies. What we actually caught that day was in strong contrast with the visionary Swallow Tail – a tiny butterfly with an undistinguished rusty top and a surprising underside in bright leaf-green, not very common in our bit of Hampshire, and appropriately called the Green Hairstreak. After flying impudently in front of our noses it insisted on settling with its wings closed, and this made it impossible to see. So Bobby and I strained our eyes trying to keep the spot in sight, convinced that we could distinguish this little scrap of green from the acres and acres of identical green all round us. We rushed across patches so wet that the mud oozed over the tops of our boots; then we crept up to where we were certain it had settled, lost sight of it, and combed the whole area, until by accident we brushed or stumbled against the plant it was on, so that it rose, a papery little bit of leaf, and went off erratically to repeat the performance. At last we managed to corner it between us on a patch of water-mint. I took it home with great care and set it – as I felt obliged – with its dull brown upperside showing, but always lifted it out on its pin to show the leaf-green underside to visitors.

In this stretch of countryside we spent a Saturday afternoon on a rising curve of excitement, catching, or at least seeing, a number of relative rarities. Neither of us had a watch and we had to guess the time, but I was ruefully conscious that I was expected back at six, and when at last we decided we really must stop and make for home, I suddenly saw in a glade holding the last of the sunlight a really superior butterfly, a White Admiral, elegant and swooping in flight, black and white on top and subtly tessellated in brown and white beneath. We had a breakneck chase among the oak trees in the evening light. I remember my mixed feelings, with the black and white butterfly, bedraggled and past its best but undoubtedly authentic, safely pinned sideways in my collecting box; I said goodbye to Bobby at the thorn gap – he had only half a mile to go to Baybridge. Then I ran the flinty mile, desperately late, my haversack bobbing uncomfortably against my side, to Cobb's Corner and anxiously down Crabbe's Hill, which seemed almost dark. My legs ached and I had a rueful conviction inside me that any punishment would be worth while for such a prize, and yet – yet, I felt a nagging worry that my mother would be genuinely anxious about me. During such small panics one reverts almost to real infancy, and I had faint visions of bloodhounds or police and ponds being dragged. I must have slowed down on the brick path – and at last plucked up courage to go through the front door into the living-room . . . Mr Toombs had arrived for an evening visit, instead of on his afternoon rounds – incredible name, incredible man. The room was full of laughter and gaiety. Bill was still up, his face a mask of chocolate, Joan with him on the sofa stuffing sweets.

I was greeted perfunctorily with only a mock horror at my lateness and warned that my own bar of chocolate cream was just going to be eaten. My relief was almost overwhelming. Mr Toombs must have had thwarted parental instincts, and as he kissed me I noticed again the clean yeasty smell of bread. He had not only arrived loaded with sweets and presents, but in the back of the van this time there were a few bottles of beer. I wondered how I had missed the conspicuous – indeed impressive – van, until I realised that it had been parked on the space behind the Shearers, perhaps for safety as it was dark, or to save lighting the lamps. Everything else was suspended when he came: my mother wasn't even knitting, and it was nearly an hour before she said, 'Arthur! *Look* at the time! Those children *must* go to bed.' And then we were pushed off, unwashed, and I took my box up to the bedroom and showed Joan the White Admiral by candlelight and got into bed, and my mother came up, happy and bright-eyed, to kiss us, but Bill was already fast asleep. We murmured for a while and heard through the floor the laughter and glugging of beer being poured into glasses, and I fell asleep thinking how really good things always come in a rush, and how my White Admiral, now lying on damp blotting paper on the top of the washstand, would look in the box, even though it had a piece out of the wing.

Near the same strip of woodland Bobby and I caught my only Purple Emperor, the one English butterfly with really 'shot' colours, purple and black, with two strange 'eyes' on the hind wings, huge and mysterious and lovely. It was not very uncommon, I had been told, in the New Forest, part of which was not far away, and I had heard from Mr Last and confirmed for myself in a book that it flew mainly around the top of oak trees and liked to feed on carrion. Bobby and I tried squashed beetles and little bits of meat from his lunch and we had sat patiently for hours under the oak trees, like Eskimos at a seal's blow-hole, ignoring the Painted Ladies that flew around us and the Graylings that tried to tempt us away. But nothing came, except flies.

One Saturday I managed to retrieve the innards of a chicken which had gone off lay and was intended for Sunday lunch. The giblets had been taken out and the rest wrapped in bloody newspaper, ready for the rubbish pit out in the Medder, and I quietly took it and put it in the haversack with my lunch. It 'gave' to my fingers like a half-blown football bladder, and smelled very odd indeed, but Bobby was thrilled, and I pretended not to be sickened. This time we put in a sunny clearing between oak trees, noted the spot, and went off for a couple of hours fruitlessly chasing other butterflies up to the top of the downs. Bobby didn't collect – his overcrowded cottage had no facilities – and at the time I was not particularly impressed by his selflessness in working so devotedly with me, Saturday after Saturday, assuming that this most delightful of occupations was delightful to him too. We went back once to the bait, but there was nothing to be seen except two sluggish violet ground beetles crawling over it, prospecting, we assumed, for burial and a good cache for the winter. We went off again, purposely dismissing it from our minds, and had our lunch – I imagined my sandwiches had a strange and distinctive taste – and we lay in the sun boasting of our prowess at this and that, chased one another down grassy slopes, ran after rabbits with sticks, and then, casually and unconcernedly, again approached the bait, which had not been out of my mind all afternoon. Settled on the little reddish goblet was – could it be? Yes, a Purple Emperor butterfly! It looked exquisite as the sun caught its iridescence. It was gently flirting its wings and imbibing some horrible juice. Bobby and I looked at each other, unable to believe our eyes, the blood rising to our faces. My hands trembled as I got my net into position, but the butterfly seemed absorbed and blind. It was a question of one long sweep across the bait and then on to the grass. Could I do it? Bobby held one hand to support me. I braced myself, swallowed, and swept the net round. For a moment I though it had got away and saw it in my mind's eye soaring majestically to the very top of the oak trees. Then the net was on the ground with the huge insect struggling inside it. Never was any offering so tenderly sacrificed as when I killed it, delicately and with commiseration. *Apatura iris*, its Latin name – I repeated over and over again as it lay with folded wings on my hand and Bobby did a war dance round me. We agreed, almost without discussion, that we should not even attempt to catch anything else that day, and I felt like taking home the chicken's guts and putting that in my collection too, out of gratitude. I spent about an hour setting the butterfly and was the hero of the school the next day when I offhandedly mentioned the matter. Even Mr Last was impressed, and *Apatura iris* was the glory of my collection until the mites got it.

The views of most adults about my obsession with collecting seemed to me irrelevant; it wasn't the Fresh Air or the Glories of Nature, nor, as my Uncle Ted declared with an aggressive air of conviction, the Thrill of the Chase. Nor was it any kind of scientific interest, but what it *was* is still unclear to me. An important part of the obsession had to do with the way in which butterflies show you their extraordinary beauties, and then immediately flutter off and vanish from sight. I wanted to enable myself to see them in detail and this was only possible when they were dead and set. Close to this was the urge to make permanent the evanescent. This feeling shaded off into a hopeless wish to order and tie down and hold and possess what in nature was erratic, chaotic, incalculable.

As I grew up a bit and began to understand more of my own feelings, I began to realise that, though greed and possessiveness and a collector's instinct were the main feelings, what I was really doing was trying to hang on to symbols, fragments, slips of what mattered most, the landscape, the place, the atmosphere. If I could have collected country smells I might have done so; I had a set of personal favourites; at one end were obvious fragrances like the heavy sickly summeriness of privet and the sweet coconut smell of gorse; at the other, subtler and more evocative juices and essences – the foetid horehound and the thin sourness of dog's mercury. In the same way I might have liked to collect sounds – the May cuckoo at sunrise for late spring, the brave song of the thrush on the ash tree to recall frosty winter days, the orchestra of grasshoppers for the July hedgerows. But I had to settle for sight and touch; so each egg, each insect, each pressed flower, evoked the particular place in which they were found – the tiny bit of swamp for ever identified with the Green Hairstreak, the wild Service tree with its flat discs of bloom solitary on the falling ground to Marwell Court, the flowery little lane leading only to the tin hut, where my cuckoo had laid in the hedge sparrow's nest.

I don't pretend that any of this was conscious or rational: I was too young to have more than the faintest feeling that the collecting was also a means to an end. The most I could ever get was a glimpse out of the corner of my eye. Through the dimness and the shadowiness I began to feel that beauty mattered, and that it was extremely fragile, like the swift's egg and the fritillary. The love I felt for the specimens in my collections seemed related obscurely to my first feelings about love and sex.

I seem to have known at least something about sex from a very early age, and probably this came from living in rural surroundings. It certainly didn't come from parental instruction; that was much later, at about twelve, when I had a brief and rather gruff monologue from my father. Then I learned the exact meaning of an expression that I had often heard earlier and still remember for its curiously nauseating use of metaphor – 'going the whole hog' – together with its undesirability except for the married. It suggested that only pigs did it, which was a strange reflection on my origin, and indeed on the behaviour of adults generally.

I twice saw a calf born and can remember rather little except for the crumpled appearance of the calf, all legs and bleat, and the immense size of the afterbirth, steaming and pink. I was surprised and rather appalled, but the experience fell into a farmyard slot, and was not connected in my mind with the more mysterious and exciting business of sex itself. With some other boys I once watched a stallion serving a mare, and what struck me was the violent agitation of the whole thing: the stallion with his immense black penis, so utterly different from the pleasant dangling one I had been familiar with in our own horse, and even more so from my own tiny affair, which seemed quite unrelated. The mare stood, apparently passive, only quivering along her flanks and looking straight forward, while the stallion, propped on her back, seemed to be moving with such desperation that his flanks were almost invisible, and he whinnied with what seemed alarm or violence rather than excitement. But to me the vision, as well as monstrous and wicked, was inherently exciting too; the other child voyeurs might all have felt it as I did, though they didn't say so. Some primal drive was perceptibly at work, though dimly and strangely, in my own body. For a long time I remembered the fast-moving savagery of the onslaught and the final desperate quiver along the stallion's back. She was a bay, and he was brown and tough, his eyes and teeth dominant; his colour seemed somehow right, and the bay's passivity alarming, only her ears pricked, as though she was being done – which I suppose in a way she was. I couldn't see why she put up with it.

My real-life experiences at that tender age were slight enough, heaven knows. Romanticism had its roots for me in the beauty and remoteness of Joan's friend Sally Hunney who sometimes met us at the shop or hovered round the cricket pitch or came blackberrying with us. She was a prototype of the traditional Hampshire child – fair to the point of whiteness, with a slide on the side of her flaxen hair, wide blue eyes, a skin that went no darker than honey in the hottest summer, and with white slightly frilly knickers, from which her long legs emerged, often with grazed or scabby knees. Being older as well as female, she adopted an attitude of infinite superiority to me, and I was grouped with Bill as 'one of the kids' for her own purposes. Her mere presence in a group of us was enough to make me feel hot and shy; once or twice she took my hand to help me up a steep hill: the heat between the trees and the heat in my heart were almost unendurable. More often she would push me and call me a silly kid or a little nit, and even being pushed by her was an honour. She would lie in the flowery fields showing those frilly knickers and gabble away to Joan about the doings of her family and her pash on Stephen Last – handsome, older, mature; but she did this with one eye on me or indeed on any other boy in earshot. How I would warm at the thought that she just might be at Cobbs' shop when I got there! My wildest dream was to kiss her, though I never did: her spindly arms and golden skin came into my dreams and symbolised splendour and beauty and the forever unattainable. She once electrified me when she said, 'Peter, I've got a bone to pick with you.' I didn't know this expression, so for me it betokened some splendid intimacy, and I was let down terribly when I discovered that it meant that she wanted to have a row – which she proceeded to do, while I blushed, stammered and was lost. Sally was beauty and love; I would no more have dreamed of boasting about her or indeed mentioning her except oh so calmly in a list of names, than I would have told Spud Newton about my most hidden fears and nightmares – the Old Man in the privy, for example.

Our kind, quiet neighbours, old Mr and Mrs Neville, moved away from Owslebury to be nearer a daughter, and their place was taken by the Mundays – a noisy lot consisting of father, mother and three children, all older than us. The two boys had already left school and were working on farms near the village. Maggie, the daughter, was flat-faced, sly, secretive and seemed to me immensely old – she was twelve. None of us like her much; she was a girl who nudged and smelt of stew. We had let the Mundays a strip of the Medder, and Maggie used it to put up a small tent made of brown blankets. One hot Friday she called to me as I fed the chickens and came close enough for the smell to become rather overpowering. She whispered that I could have something worth my while for a whole packet of wine gums if I went to the tent on Saturday afternoon – her brothers would be haymaking, she said, and her mother 'Up the Institute'. Although I disliked her and was frightened of her, I was also fascinated by her maturity and knowingness. So I spent my weekly pocket money on wine gums, resisted the considerable temptation to have at least a taste, and after dinner when Arthur went to play cricket and Joan and Florence were safely busy in the scullery, I crept with nervous backward looks towards the low brown tent. She was there, sweltering in the heat, arms and legs akimbo, dark greasy hair spread, a sly grin on her face. 'Got the wine gums, Pete?' she asked, and I passed them into her hand. She stuffed one into her mouth and said, 'Come on then.' She had no knickers on and was already faintly hairy. I was terrified out of my life. 'You're supposed to get on top, but you're only a kid . . . Don't you want to?' I wanted to and didn't want to. Her armpits were slightly hairy too, and the sweat and onion smells were overpowering. She kissed me and it was mixed with wine-gum flavour. 'Take off your shorts and you can put it in if you want to – I don't mind,' she said devastatingly. 'Come on, you little funk!' She took another wine gum from the wrappings and packed it into her cheeks. 'About time you grew up!' I had to get away. When she fumbled with my shorts I pretended my mother was calling me, planted a kiss on the dark cheek and wriggled backwards out of the tent. I felt very hot indeed. It was clearly forbidden, exciting, repulsive and above all to be escaped from. I boasted about it to my closest male friends at school, not altogether truthfully. I secretly thought that she embodied the dark side of life, like the spiders in the bedrooms, Ernie Bone, and the woman with a goitre hanging six inches below her chin. So the sweating stallion, and Maggie Munday and Spud Newton's accounts of his doings became a continuity. I didn't know all the words, but I knew the feelings: lust, sex, copulation, were all about me. Only Sally Hunney was sacrosanct, a secret, a wonder and a wild desire.

By the end of August the butterfly population had thinned out and I was reduced to the relatively clodhopper substitute of moths. On these my feelings were mixed. The Hawk Moths with their long, thin, sharp-angled wings were exciting enough for anybody, but apart from the Eyed and Poplar Hawks, which were common in the area and therefore less thrilling, there was not much prospect of catching any. My reactions were in any case a bit mixed – hawk moths were so enormous they made me feel small. Once in the patch of sapling beeches beyond Frankie Southgate's cottage when I was with Joan, she let out a stifled shriek. There, on the back of her middle finger, clinging, was a Death's Head Hawk Moth, presumably recently hatched, its body longer than her finger, 'Take it off, Pete!' she kept saying as she covered her face with her other hand to shut out the fearsome sight, 'Take it *off*!'

'Look at the skull, Joan, the skull between the wings. Isn't it gorgeous? – and it's quite rare, too.' When I told her it might squeak if disturbed she was even more horrified and tried hard to shake it off, but it clung firmly, embracing her finger with its furry legs. By now I was half thrilled and half frightened, for her and for myself, it was so huge – five inches across the wings. I began to remember stories I'd heard about the Death's Head which I only half disbelieved: this one was being so devoted to us that superstitious stories began to seem real. At length I managed to persuade it to let go and we knocked it off on to the dog's mercury below, and went home quickly, Joan shuddering uncontrollably and longing to give Florence a blow-by-blow account. But though I returned at once with the killing bottle the vast moth had vanished.

But hawk moths were not common, and what we saw much more often were the confusing brownish-grey clumsy moths belonging to the large family of the *Noctuids*, or the even larger and mostly duller family of the *Geometrids*. None of these moths pleased me visually, but my greed was undiminished. One evening I persuaded my father to help me 'sugar' a tree trunk on the edge of the Medder; this meant dabbing or painting it with a mixture of treacle and stale beer – the latter a rare commodity. This mixture was supposed to be irresistible to most of the moths in creation so I had a restless night dreaming of the tree smothered with drunken insects. Soon after dawn I walked across the wet grass in my nightshirt to inspect it, and was disappointed to find only two bedraggled Cinnabar moths, which were ten a penny during the day.

I recognised and liked only a few conspicuous moths, most of them not all that different from butterflies, in being fresh, glamorous and above all creatures of daylight – things like the vivid Tiger Moths and the beautiful Emerald. My bible on the subject of insects, Kirby's *Butterflies and Moths of the United Kingdom*, with its 432 pages and its 70 plates, was the source of both confusion and disappointment. The book had a broken spine and was a present from Mr Last. It was far too technical for me; its plates had Roman figures, so I could be looking for Plate LXVII and figure 28 (*Hydrocampa stagnata* – The Beautiful China Mark). The volume was also far too heavy, though I often tried to consult it or browse through it on the sofa. Most depressing were the dozens and dozens of plates illustrating hundreds of things that were just moths – brown or brownish, all different and yet irritatingly similar. Checking with care my few home-caught specimens against the coloured pictures was always going to be a great thrill, and always turned out a great bore. When I found a picture identical with my dead moth, smallish and brownish, I would look it up with difficulty, in the latinised text, and then, as like as not, it would say the Brindled Wainscot or some such, and inform me that it was rare or local in the north-west of England, or only known from one fen in East Anglia. So it couldn't be that, but it was exactly like it; and no other plate, as I laboriously hunted through the over-heavy book, showed anything in the least resembling it – unless it turned out to be this dreary Turnip Moth which is 'common throughout Britain', but I'd got one already and it didn't really look the same anyhow.

The only entirely satisfactory thing about moths was their wonderful English names, which I found surprising as well as delightful. Listed alphabetically at the end of Kirby's book there were romantic names like the Willow Beauty, the Peach Blossom and the Ghost Moth; comic ones like the Mouse, the Dingy Footman and the Beautiful Snout; and a very large group of mysterious if not unintelligible names like the Suspected Moth, the Northern Spinach, the Tabby Knothorn, and, most impenetrable of all, the Plumeless Plume. Even Joan and Florence, whose indifference to the insect world surprised me, found some of these names charming, and once or twice had me recite them to visitors as a party piece.

We had a fair number of moths in the cottage in August and September even if they weren't invited, but now my mother agreed to let me open the windows and attract them into the scullery by the light of one of the oil lamps while she stayed in the sitting-room with Joan; Bill had gone to bed after playing with Teddy Chenery. It was a muggy evening in September, and, having assured myself that the door into the sitting-room was tightly shut, I drew back the curtains, opened the window, and sat and waited. I wanted to stay mobile, so instead of having my feet imprisoned inside the rim of the downside-up table, I sat sideways with my feet on one of the goatskin rugs, and watched the oil lamp which I had put on the table below the window. As I sat there I worried about having only a single killing bottle, as many moths have thick bodies and unlike most butterflies couldn't be killed by a quick squeeze. A few which had normal, rather dull males, like the Spring Usher or the Winter Moth, had wingless females that were horridly like spiders. If any of these appeared I should do my best to ignore them.

Still, who knew what tonight might bring? Surreptitiously I put some black treacle out on a saucer temptingly near the lamp, and sat again to watch what aliens might appear. The first arrivals included two bluebottles, some craneflies and an orange-bodied sawfly – a disgusting creature that sleeps upside-down suspended from the ceiling by one leg. These were followed by the tiny impalpable moths that I called clothes moths, wisps of greyish white that turned themselves into minute slivers of matchstick as soon as they settled. And then, from the scented, still, velvet of the garden and perhaps from the great fields and woods beyond, the moths began to blunder in. A Yellow Underwing arrived friskily, a stout coarse moth; and then almost immediately, another – but when I was able to inspect it closely, I discovered that it was delightfully and subtly different. The first was Broad-

Bordered with a black funereal edging to the lower wing, the second Narrow-Bordered, with an appropriately narrower border and charmingly marked with a dark dash on the corner of the upper wing. Next came an Ermine Moth, snowy white on the wings, with a hairy thorax and elegantly flicked with black; two Goldtails and a Whitetail, and a large swooping Pepper-and-Salt moth. During the evening more than one huge Oak Eggar with a masterful flight dashed itself rather savagely against the glass of the lamp, and finally folded itself neatly into a brown tube like a cigar stub on the white oilcloth of the scullery table. My mother called out to ask whether I was all right and I shushed her as if her voice would frighten my guests. Rather alarmingly a large black flapping lump arrived and hurled itself aimlessly at the walls and chairs and at me and finally went to rest near the ceiling to reveal itself as a moth called the Old Lady – a very rusty old lady in funeral black. A Red Underwing was a tremendous excitement, as I hadn't ever seen a live one, with its lichened forewings and bright brick-red black-edged underwings – large and beautiful and undamaged. Perpetually greedy as I was, the arrival of the Red Underwing set me dreaming that as the Underwing family was obviously favouring me this evening there would soon arrive the biggest and last, as it were, of the Underwing hierarchy – the Clifden Nonpareil, with exquisite ashen-grey top wings and the underwing a subtle blue with a black rim. Though it was a 'rare insect' according to Kirby, the caterpillar fed on ash, and there was an ash tree a few yards away, so I thought it was quite reasonable to expect it . . . but it didn't come.

Anyway, within half an hour the place seemed alive with moths from a quarter of an inch to three inches across. I stood up to walk round the walls with my coloured plates, the goatskin rug crackling bumpily as I did so. But the doubtful ones all seemed to have settled outside the bright circle of light cast by my lamp on the ceiling; in the dark they looked as dim as any Turnip Moth, and probably were. I had handy my cyanide killing bottle, and it was a question of putting it over a moth spreadeagled on the wall, in the hope that the fumes would kill it, only to find after a long wait holding the jar with an aching wrist, that the moth had plenty of life as it dashed off to more roundabouts and dodgems near the lamp. By this time the treacle saucer was full of sawflies trying to get out, or in. There were more moths than a whole entomological society could deal with, and I had thirty-four either torpid or dead, some still flapping feebly in the killing bottle, some put ready for identification in the morning in a relaxing box, some – far too many, really – still awaiting attention on the walls and the table. Then I was called really firmly for bed as it was after nine-thirty, and my mother and Joan had tea things and food in the sitting-room so that they didn't have to venture back into the scullery. I was to blow out the lamp, leaving the window wide open so that the moths would go out again at dawn – which I rather doubted. My relaxing box full of game and my killing bottle must be taken back into the museum under the eaves in the dark and 'For heaven's sake shut the door after you!' They didn't want my safari extended to the quiet snugness of the sitting-room with its smell of home-made cigarettes and cosy domesticity. And in the morning, sure enough, when I got up early and crept down, stepping over the well-known creaky fourth stair, the cold scullery *was* empty of moths, though there were an alarming number of flies, daddy-long-legs, and spiders still around, and a treacle saucer so jammed up with craneflies and sawflies that I thought it best to throw all the contents in the ditch under the nettles, and I wiped the saucer rather roughly on the long wet grass. After breakfast I would spend the morning identifying and setting the moths – and where on earth they were all to go I didn't know. But I used the time before breakfast to cut many shaky strips of tracing paper and to sort out the right sizes of pins.

The moth-hunt or moth-trap didn't happen again, partly because of the *embarras de richesse*, and partly because it wasn't popular in the household; Joan didn't care for the larger ones, and we all thought that a generalised crawler-magnet might encourage spiders. What it perhaps provided, more than just the moths for my collection, was a sense of the vast complex of night-life outside, looking in as it were, and indeed coming in, as guests or victims.

CHAPTER FIFTEEN

PRECARIOUS HOLIDAY

It was the last morning before we left for a late holiday in London. Our parents, to my surprise and delight, were allowing us to be away from school in October – something to do with my father's work – and we were to stay not at Inverness Terrace but at his own lodgings in Aldersgate. This word evoked the image of a large gate made of alder wood; but it was also one of a series of place names frequently used by my father which called to mind powerful, romantic, yet vague pictures of a teeming Dickensian London – *Great Expectations* was my authority for this: Holborn (mysterious spelling, mysterious pronunciation), Fleet Street, Ludgate Hill, Chancery Lane. These were the areas where my father was presumably in his glory – unsmiling, slightly high-coloured, knowing everywhere and everyone, and living in a world of cigars and sherry.

I was allowed out on this morning from the end of breakfast till 11.30 a.m., while Florence and Joan packed and Bill drew, and I was lent Joan's wristwatch which I kept in my jacket pocket as the strap didn't have a hole far enough in to fit my wrist. I took my net and collecting box with me, and decided to walk along past the tin house on Gough's Lane and out to the Field of the Runcible Cow. As I went down the narrow front path I brushed against the Michaelmas daisies, unexciting at the best of times, but now sad-looking objects with papery brown leaves and fluffy seedheads. The plums were long over, and the leaves were yellowing patchily, twig by twig. As I got out on to the road, I saw that the birches which flanked the end of the garden were still green at the top, but in the centre of the trees the leaves were a clear fine yellow. Many of these lay in a neat runnel where the wind had blown them into the verges. The hedge colours had changed too; behind the long bents of dead grassheads there were blackish dogwood berries, the two kinds of bryony, both of which had splendid juicy-looking clusters of scarlet fruits, and the traveller's joy carried its grey fluffs billowing over the hawthorns and elders. I turned the corner on to the track where there was an old tree festooned with ivy, blooming in elegant discs of yellow-green flowers, and I stood watching in the weak sun for any unusual late butterflies, perhaps a Comma or – who knows? – an Elephant Hawk Moth. But there was nothing except two Red Admirals and a Peacock flirting their wings and sunning their colours. It would be good to catch something and set it before we left for London, as the season really would be over by the time we got back.

Further down the lane, beyond the deserted tin house, which was painted in a colour close to what my water-colour box showed as Hooker's Deep Green, was a large patch of arable weed on a rubbish heap. This had been a good source of bits of china for the Medder Stores and a good area for summer butterflies, but now it was dominated by the fleshy and unexciting stinking goosefoot, which no self-respecting butterfly would go near even if it hadn't been heavy with green seed. The flints on the pathway glistened black and grey against the white chalk, and Cabbage Whites still fluttered aimlessly about. I thought back to the summer days of the butcher-bird and the Silver-washed Fritillaries and the long cut-and-carted sainfoin, and wished it was still happening. Kicking at flints, I dawdled on to where the path ran through a flattish neglected field full of ragwort, but as usual the flowerheads carried only an occasional late cinnabar moth. I could hear the yellowhammer monotonously repeating its song which didn't sound to me in the least like 'A little bit of bread and no che-e-e-e-se', and three larks were climbing loudly in the still blue sky.

Suddenly on a tussocky bit of field I saw an orange-pink butterfly with a strong flight dipping over a few remaining thistles – *Vanessa cardui*, the Painted Lady. Not wildly exciting, but I wanted a female underside, and should have to catch it to see which sex it was. So I chased the quick-moving insect over and round very prickly thistles. At last it settled on one of them where a few purple petals still remained among the grey hair-combings of the seedheads, and I managed to sweep my net over and round it, tearing the muslin slightly on the spines but landing the Painted Lady on the bumpy field. It fluttered madly as I worked my hands from the metal circle up to the end, only to find that the insect was unquestionably male – beautiful still and fresh-looking, but not what I wanted. So I turned the net upwards and hoped as I saw it sweep away that I hadn't damaged its wings. Not a good morning, really; but at least here were some fine-looking blackberries only slightly palisaded by nettles, and the stick of my butterfly net came in handy to pull the arcs down to my level. There was no point in saving them – I had no container, and in any case they were past their best, and we were off before dinner-time. So I ate them and in due course felt better, and walked to the Field of the Runcible Cow with my tongue playing away at the backs and crevices of my teeth where pips had lodged.

I scrambled through a hedge, the line of which cut across my path. It was full of honeysuckle, the red and yellow blossoms now replaced by neat stumpy groups of sticky red berries. I then came to the field and climbed the heavy stile that led into it, though no one in living memory had ever seen the footpath that ought to have led from it. There were dry-topped cowpats in the hedge angle, and they were crawling with small sluggish brown-red flies. I walked up the slope to the patch of gorse, elder and hawthorn. In places you could actually walk under the gorse bushes. From below they were black, sere and apparently dead, though some yellow blossoms survived on the highest of the tips above. Here the linnets and goldfinches nested and I had searched for the Dartford Warbler. I loved this patch of bushes, as it felt secret like an outdoor house with me underneath, but it lacked the spring splendour of being also a quarry for nests. Now there was nothing better than battered remnants. I put my hand into one or two above my head, vaguely hoping that there might be bits of eggshell left, but I found only dry leaves and a couple of hawthorn berries resting on the damp horsehair. I wondered if I ought to be home helping with the packing, but felt I had been sent rather than allowed out, so that presumably was all right. I felt a bit aimless; I found some more blackberries, watched a pair of goldfinches on the thistle seeds, and then struck back to the path further on. To my surprise I met Leslie Binder with his fair-haired mother carrying a wicker basket as usual. They seemed not only polite to me, but charmingly warm and friendly; they told me they were going to a pasture behind Farmer Gale's where there were said to be still plenty of field mushrooms. I arranged with Leslie to visit him when I got back from London, and to go chestnuting in a grove down the cart-lane past his house. They went off, cool and unsweaty in spite of their continual busy collecting of everything useful; for myself I preferred the useless and vulnerable beauty of my few eggs and butterflies to their perpetual bottling, wine-making, drying, preserving, pickling, chutney-making – a houseful of usefulness.

Everywhere around me there were seedheads. The scrambling vetches had black off-centre stars, the dogroses were yellow-leaved and bright-hipped, the hawthorn umbels were nearly red, the nightshade had fine black clusters like small grapes, and the mallow seedheads reminded me of the game in the Medder Shop so long ago. One side of the hedge was hot in the strengthening sun, the other cool, damp and almost spring-like with a few harebells at its foot, and there were elaborate slabby spiderwebs still holding dew as well as the cartwheel ones with the small speckly monsters suspended in the middle. I picked a sloe and sucked it, and the juice immediately dried out my saliva. I wondered how anyone could make wine out of such sourness, but guessed that the Binders would. Then Joan's watch said 11.15 a.m., and I quickened my step. Now from a little bump in the path I could just see the chimney of the cottage, and as I drew level with my three thorn bushes, some way off up the slope, I saw them oddly end-on, but still implying richly that this was home. There was no one visible or audible at Frankie Southgate's, and only a whistling in the bar at the Shearers. But back in the cottage a pretty clean sweep seemed to have been made. Two ancient portmanteaus and an old leather suitcase were strapped or fastened; there were a couple of cardboard boxes tied with string and a pile of coats, scarves, gloves, a handbag, haversacks. This time we were having a taxi, and it was soon due; so I paid a last visit to My Museum to check that everything was in order and that neither thieves nor predators had been stealing my White Admiral or undermining my shrike's egg while I had been out on my walk. All was well, though still dusty, and the door creaked as I shut it and put down the clacking wooden latch.

I hadn't even time to wash before the rubber-and-horn honk announced the arrival of the taxi – THE taxi, indeed, from Twyford. The driver very quickly piled our shabby bags on the space next to his box-shaped driving cab and fastened them all down firmly with built-in straps, distorting our cardboard boxes a bit in the process. A last quick stare round the cottage sitting-room revealed only Florence's matches. The key was given to Mrs Munday next door, and she waved us off as we drove down the narrow road past the Shearers and up Jackman's Hill. To Morestead, to Twyford, to Winchester, to London, to Aldersgate! The excitement was tremendous, though faintly coloured with regret at leaving My Museum and the Owslebury countryside for a while.

It was getting dusk, or rather foggy, by the time we reached my father's lodgings – No. 20, Lever Street, Aldersgate – and how different from what I had envisaged, though equally exciting. The narrow-fronted house was built like its neighbours of blackish-red brick, with stone-coloured window surrounds, and a well-scrubbed doorstep which impressed me by being actually *on* the pavement and within a few feet of a street lamp exactly like the one at Morestead Church. We knocked on the door with the black lion-headed knocker, and were admitted by a large man who turned out to be Mr Mullins. He worked for the railway and was a burly man with more necks at the back than at the front – bald, cheerful and smelling as if his clothes were saturated with engine oil or the chlorine-tasting smoke I so loved at Paddington Station. He talked cockney of a breadth and width I had never previously heard; I found it fascinating but hard to follow. Like Grandpa Hewett's house, this one had rooms so stuffed with furniture that you had to watch your edges every second between going up the front steps and actually sitting or lying down. My father had a bed-sitting-room at the top of the stairs. It was dominated by an enormously high double bed with spotless brass knobs on the head-support, and covered with a thick eiderdown decorated with gargantuan flowers, which I admired. This fat bed rose from a sea of rag rugs of great thickness and complexity. If you slipped or scuffed even slightly you brought down the spindly-legged stool which served as a bedside table. This touchingly carried a wedding photograph of Florence in an oxidised silver frame, as well as a round-cornered tin with the familiar tobacco, orange-covered cigarette papers and damp dead fag-ends. There was a small deal table by the window with Owslebury-type impedimenta of cardboard and paintpots, which also struck a familiar note.

Everything else was strange. On arrival we had to light the gas because the fog – a surprisingly yellow fog of a kind I had never seen before – was already hanging round the street. There were two brackets, one at each side of the mirror above the fireplace, and my father found them hard to light with a match which burnt his fingers before the loud hiss turned into a humming brightness. Two wood-and-leather armchairs backed with lace and piled with rugs and cushions embraced my father and mother, who smoked and talked while we finished our bag of Owslebury apples, though supper was imminent.

Soon Mrs Mullins called up the stairs, 'Mr Uit – if yer ready?' and we all had a quick wash in Arthur's rather splendid gold and blue basin which sat on its own doily on a washstand in the corner. There were miniature doilies for the holed soap bowl and the hair-tidy, and even a third on which stood a little china tree with branches for hanging rings on; I wondered whether the latter was much use to my father, but no one bothered to explain that this was a lodging room for either sex. Mrs Mullins made a great drama of placing us round the scrubbed deal table downstairs; we were squashed against the wall or backed against the chiffonier, with lumpy cushions thoughtfully provided on the chair seats, which made our balance a bit uncertain. She was in black with grey trimmings and had a shelf-like bosom which started at her collar bones. She had gingery hair, smoked incessantly, talked faster than anyone I have ever met, and could modulate from one syllable to the next, between a cooing, soothing voice she thought appropriate for me and Bill, and a sudden terrifying bellow: 'Charleen! Issat you? Bring the beer in ere, quick! Oh that child will be the def o me yit.' Charleen, a handsome and well-built but rather sulky teenage girl, brought in a large white jug foaming at the top and said, 'Pleezeter meecher' to each of us before putting it in the middle of the table and vanishing again. Then I heard for the first time the immortal words, bellowed rather than screamed to Mr Mullins who was outside in the washhouse or lav: 'Farver! Yer supper's poured out!' And in came Farver, still smelling of glass-domed stations and thrilling journeys, and handed my father a glass of foxy-red beer with a creamy froth. 'Glad to ave yer ere,' he said, and Arthur said, 'Glad to *be* heah,' in a faintly posher voice, I thought, than his normal one. Then the faggots, the suspiciously green and almost mashed peas, and the crumbly potatoes were proudly brought in, and we shyly accepted second helpings until we were glowing with exertion and satisfied hunger. Florence was beginning to relax and Bill's eyes were rapidly glazing over.

It was agreed that after the long sticky journey from Owslebury we children should have baths, and Mrs Mullins said many times while we picked at the roly-poly pudding that the copper had been alight since midday so there was plenty of water. Despite a family superstition that baths after food were medically dubious, Bill and I were to have our bath at once and be got to bed. So the Mullinses and Arthur went out into the washhouse/bakehouse, which was separate from the house itself, while Bill and I were undressed, and then put into overcoats and plimsolls, which we thought very odd. It was very strange to be taken, dressed like this, hand in hand with Florence, through a few feet of slowly swirling yellow fog; in Owslebury we were always bathed in front of the sitting-room fire. The fog quickly got round your knees and into your cold crotch as well as your throat, and the yellow was intensified by a faint glow from the street lamps on the pavement of Lever Street. There were only two lamps, and Mrs Mullins regarded it as a mark of distinction to have one outside her very front door 'so yer didn ave to grope yer way back at night arter a pint at the Bricklayers, it was of a convenience.' I was mystified by the steam-engine smell of the fog and even more by the washhouse. It was built at right angles to the house; the bulk of it was brick, but the front was of caulked timber, with an ill-fitting pair of half-doors to get in by. Inside, wonder of wonders, there was a fire – a coal fire, glowing red. It was an astonishing thing to find in an outhouse, we thought, until we realised how very natural it was: how else would you heat a copper? The only light apart from the glow from the fire was a hurricane lantern, and this made the scene wild and strange. We took off our coats and plimsolls. Our fronts were warm, though the cold, wind and fog seemed to bite into our backs from the cracks between the half-doors. But the water in the brown and white hipbath was nice and hot, and as we were soaped and rubbed by Florence the pleasure and strangeness seemed complete.

Mrs Mullins had put out her own towels, 'me barf taals. Farver give em to me fer ahr twentyfith – two on em. No, yer welcome. Keep them littleuns o' yourn warm – that barf ahse ainarf cold even this time of year. When the real winter come it don' bear finken of. Farver goes dahn the Municipal and I make do in the front room till abaht Easter time.'

In these fine big blue and white towels we were patted and dried. When I was finished I stepped sideways, and slid on the still wet tablet of soap – and discovered as I sprawled on the floor that it was of very hard tiles with runnels between, highly appropriate to a washhouse. But I was only slightly bruised, and, glowing from the bath, Bill and I were led back happily enough across the yard, now pitch-dark except for the foggy hovering glow above. The hall and stairway were cold, and we were bundled quickly up into a bedroom which had been specially made up for the three of us. There was another vast high brass bedstead for Bill and me which you had literally to climb up into; it was covered with an elaborate crochet bedspread and smelt half and half of carbolic and lavender. Joan was to come up later and occupy a sort of camp-bed as near the floor as we were near the ceiling. There was only a very narrow channel of threadbare carpet between it and the monster we were to sleep in. Bill fell asleep instantly once Florence took the candle away, and I stayed awake a little while looking at the yellow glow outside the window and hearing the approaching and fading clanks and hums of the trams out on the main road at right angles to ours. I thought with pleasure of sleeping in a flat-faced terrace of houses with two street lamps – one ours, one for the rest of the road. Before I dropped off I heard a short symphony, or quartet at least, of cats, a man's voice raised in anger, and the distant sound of broken glass.

The next few days – a week or two – are confused in my memory. They were excitingly empty of school, and soon got filled with activities, including a good deal of travel by tube and bus to visit relatives, mostly by day and therefore with Florence but not Arthur. I liked the escalators, though there was a hint of desperation, or now-or-neverness, about the jump back to terra firma at top and bottom. I loved the masses of advertisements – black print on yellow, black on pink; elegant flat-chested ladies drinking Wincarnis; men in immaculate evening dress smoking De Reske, a neat tube at 45° in their mouths, a thin wisp ascending. I enjoyed the way my change was slapped down on the metal counter when I was allowed to buy tickets. Even better was the throat-clearing sound made by the new automatic machines before they delivered my ticket like a green tongue stuck half-way out; then the whole procedure was delightedly gone through again for Joan's, and Bill's, and Florence's. I relished the hot ozone smell in the station, even the fag-ends and bits of newspaper blowing with the up-draught when the train noise rose, grew, shouted, roared and bellowed as the train dashed into the station. Still better was the noise of the doors hissing shut and the brakes tuning up – sounds I soon learned to imitate. Some of our journeys were on the old Met. with separate brass handles for each carriage and an entrancing way of taking us from the dark innards of the earth to the foggy daylight. There were bus noises and glimpses of the Thames, before we went back again to the hot dark. All this I found fascinating.

We soon learned to shop locally – first, I think, with Charleen, who had a childish streak as well as a capacity for leadership; perhaps she was fourteen rather than sixteen. We shopped for both families, so I clutched a list of things in Florence's familiar handwriting, while Charleen carried a scruffy bit of grey paper with ill-spelt and often indecipherable words written very closely together with a blunt pencil stub by Mrs Mullins. The days seemed always bleak and cold, and sometimes wet as well, or misty; strangely it seemed warmer at dusk with the fog and the steaming wagon-horses, than during the morning's shopping. It was interesting to go to different shops for different classes of things, and a whole shop devoted to selling vegetables was a novelty. At the greengrocer's we bought white turnips with green caps, warty swedes in purple and brown with a little caked earth on the injured patches, carrots, some whole, some fissured and split, and a few small onions with the curved strawy skins loosening from their hard oval bodies – all this was twopennorth of 'potherbs' for the frequent stews. At the grocers, which had a counter full of showcards that might well have been designed by Arthur, we got flour for dumplings and treacle puddings, and watched the sugar being weighed out on tall brass-and-marble balances. It was poured into a metal scoop and thence into a firm blue bag which it filled and bellied out as the bag turned scoop by scoop from square to roundish, until finally the top was folded into place intricately with consummate neatness. Even tea was served loose, from actual tea-chests with silver paper frilling the edges, and sold in brown packages. Further down the road was the chemists, distinguished by three huge exquisitely clear bottles high up in the window – a vivid rose-red, a clear strong but transparent blue, like the Owslebury skies on a good July day, a yellow like bright lemonade, all topped by stoppers like vast raindrops; the bottles themselves looked, even in the dim light of the bleak morning, like giant earrings. Here we bought a string of semi-medicines, tonics, strengtheners, backache pills, cough cures, mainly for Mrs Mullins, who made her body a depository for all the patent medicines of the period. This was to our advantage, as we liked the little shop with its two steps down and the brisk greeting of a white-coated shopkeeper of alarming cleanliness who smelled strongly of paregoric. At the newsagent's on the corner we bought Mrs Mullins her 'book' – *Woman's Weekly*. This had a cover printed in blue, showing sometimes a young heroine with a slide in her permed hair, looking either winsome or heavy-hearted, and sometimes a more mature female proudly displaying her knitted twinset. The butcher, in his sawdust-floored shop, looked cold, his hands pink and chapped, his apron bloody even early in the morning, as if he'd been killing and slicing since dawn. I stared at his wooden chopping-board, shaped more like a cake of soap than a cube, the result of being scrubbed and hacked on for so long. He used his chopper to split the bones of our breast of lamb before he rolled it in three or four sheets of newspaper, which were eagerly read later by Charleen and her mother through its splodges of blood and slivers of fat and bone. Behind him hung alarmingly an upside-down sheep which still had a woolly head and real eyes instead of being anonymous meat. Sometimes there was also a hare or two, bleeding through the nose into a little metal cup – a sad fate for a creature so beautifully furred, its white and fox-brown so subtly modulated and shaded into itself, and so reminiscent of the fields of home. Still, it was a passing pang.

Where the road widened there was often a street market, and here we bought kippers from a stall which Joan wouldn't go near, but to which Bill and I were drawn in fascinated loathing. It had a couple of metal trays, one of which contained live eels, dark mussel-shelled blue with bright eyes. They slimed and squirmed gently together and made knotty patterns against one another – very live in contrast to the very dead crabs and herrings and triangular bits of pink skate elsewhere on the stall. Very live, that is, until one of the shapeless moustached old ladies who seemed to haunt the market, asked for a pound of eels. The stall-holder groped with his scaly and fishy left hand into the tray, pulled out two or three slimy eels which were suddenly galvanised into twisting violent movement, and put them on the scales. Occasionally he replaced one of the squirmers by a smaller or bigger one, till the weight was right. Then with his right hand he picked up a knife honed to a razor sharpness, tipped the wriggling eels on to his bloodied block and cut their heads off with a single sharp stroke, leaving the eye still bright, and the long, sinuous body still twisting, even when he sliced it into two-inch bloody segments. I had seen my share of such shocking sights in the village farmyards, but the remorseless accuracy, and, it seemed, bloodthirsty cruelty of this made my heart beat faster and my eyes pop with disbelief. Even the newspaper bundle was throbbing and quivering a bit as the old woman inside the bundle of coats took it and put it in her basket. So shopping, if not edifying, had its fascinations for an eight year old, and my chin and Bill's were close enough to the eels' sudden recognition of the knife for the whole experience to be very close to our own necks and our wincing hearts.

It was more fun to roam the streets in the charge of Joan or Charleen. My dominant impression was of the total 'otherness' of the lives of these East Londoners. I had been dimly aware on walks from the bus stop that not many minutes from Inverness Terrace a very different life was being led from the splendours of my grandfather's house – hard, dark and overpopulated; but now I was in the middle of it. We played cricket against a brick wall in Lever Street with boys whose hair was clipped to the skull except for a front quiff like the flap of an envelope. Astonishingly, many of them were without boots and had very tough and dirty feet – as anyone would have on those wet and muddy pavements. I soon found an outlet for my collecting instincts in this birdless, flowerless, insectless area, and began collecting bus tickets, which were coloured differently for each value. The object – as in the Medder Shop – was 'variety in uniformity': to get a firm square wedge of identical white penny tickets, green three ha'penny ones and so on; and as with stamps, the difficult ones were the odd values – the fivepenny orange, the ninepenny violet, the elevenpenny gray. One evening my father knocked together a conductor's board with elastic neatly stapled to both sides, so that I could put my tickets tightly into each 'compartment', and Bill and I could play buses. But as with all my collecting activities, there was mild annoyance in the unfairness of the world as represented by an overflow of tuppennies and only three elevenpennies which were liable to slip out of the elastic. Finding the more interesting tickets lodged against shop counters or damply lying in the gutter was gratifying. But the rarest ones would surely be torn or grimy, and forays into the cobbled road with its traffic bumbling past were dangerous even if sometimes rewarding. In this setting the horses smelled rural; they were often in pairs, all nostrils and ringing hooves, and clattered along at a smart trot, their vans or carts defined by bright brass lamps on either side of the wrapped-up driver. Round these large creaking structures, dozens of bicycles rushed by, some swerving dangerously across their bows. Still vivid to me are the throat-catching smell of the yellow fog while I held tight on to a fivepenny ticket without creasing it, the indignant clanging of the swaying lighted tramcars (which had rather dull white tickets for all prices), the chasing round lamp-posts of shouting quiffed barefoot boys, the newspaper man on the corner and the rag-and-bone dealer crying his wares.

Twice in the afternoon we went to a cinema. I think it was called The Majestic Kinema; anyway it had naked electric light bulbs round its name to give it glamour. The posters outside showed villains with green faces, heroines of transcendental beauty with little scarlet bow mouths and frizzy hair, and a strong-jawed hero with a pencil-line moustache duelling simultaneously with six slit-eyed undersized criminals. Everything about the place was enchanting. A lady with a cigarette in a tiny triangular box gave us 'Three fourpennies' and the tickets issued from the machine on the desk like a string of sausages, still pink but squashed flat. A beautiful usherette who also sold ice-creams admitted us by lifting a dusty curtain and led us with her torch down a sharpish slope to our seats near the front. The auditorium smelled of cigarettes and cachous; the tip-up seats made a groaning squeak as we sat in them, and Joan got out her sweets and settled herself for a long happy afternoon of sucking and watching. Two or three times during the afternoon the usherette sprayed the whole place with something I thought smelled delicious but was probably a disguised insecticide – these little cinemas weren't called fleapits for nothing.

I can't really remember the films themselves except that they were either desperately exciting and frightening, terribly sad so that all three of us had a little weep, or – best of all – wildly funny. When the lights went up there were queues for ice-cream or, rather, disorderly bunches surrounding the harassed usherette. Kids climbed over the backs of the seats to greet friends, to get a better view, or just for the hell of it. When the Big Pikcher started even the rowdiest hushed. The darkness was almost palpable, and when we emerged, sad that it was over but emotionally replete, the haloed street lights and lit-up shop fronts outside seemed remote and unreal in comparison with the womblike warmth of the cinema.

I should have been quite content if this régime had gone on much longer – it seemed so colourful, fascinating, absorbing. But one evening Joan called Bill and me in from playing in the street and told us that my father was back early from work as he had something important to tell us.

We three settle down side by side in a slightly apprehensive row on the high bed, our feet dangling. Florence seems a trifle anxious, and Arthur, as always when a 'scene' is coming up, looks more serious than usual. Both light cigarettes. The tension is palpable: what on earth are they going to say? Is Grandma Jennings dead? Or Grandpa Hewett? Or has Arthur lost his job? Are we all going to the workhouse? I swallow and there is a gap where my breathing should be. Joan is a bit flushed, but Bill obviously doesn't know what's going on any more than I do.

Arthur takes a drag, clears his throat noisily. 'I have to tell you three children something which you may not like, but upon which we have decided entirely on your behalf and for your benefit. Joan is due to take her scholarship and, as she is clever, she will in all probability go to a good school. I think you all know that there is no school in Owslebury suitable for her talents – nowhere, in fact, nearer than Winchester.'

'And that's five miles away, and how could Joan possibly get there and back every day?' Florence cuts in.

'I'll thank you not to interrupt, please Florence,' says my father with suitable gravity and dignity. Florence subsides, looks chastened. I steal a glance at Joan, who colours up a bit more and looks strangely dignified at her commendation, but at the same time uncomfortable about the rebuke addressed to Florence.

'Your Mother and I have thought long and seriously about this problem,' Arthur continues solemnly. 'You know that we have had financial difficulties, and life has not always been easy. We have decided that the rail fare from Paddington to Winchester weekly is a drain on our present resources, and we can no longer afford to keep up what are to all intents and purposes two establishments, one here at Lever Street and one at the cottage, with all the expenditure, etc. etc. etc. and so on and so forth.'

There is a pause and my heart misses a beat, my swollen heart.

'I'm sorry to say, therefore, that we have decided that we must live in London, and,' he swallows a bit, 'you three children and your mother will not be returning to Owslebury.'

My heart misses another beat. 'What about my museum?' I yelp. 'What about all my eggs and butterflies and the chickens and my stamp album? What about Bunty?' I begin to cry, hopelessly, and Florence rushes across, kneels and holds me close to her.

'You *must* try not to grizzle and upset your mother, Peter,' says my father, in an unsmiling way which makes me feel worse. 'I'm ashamed of you. Do you imagine it has been easy for us? We shall have your collections sent on. Bunty is to stay with the Chenerys and will be much happier there than he could conceivably be in London. The chickens are already sold and the little furniture we had in the cottage is being sold or given away. You can safely leave such practical problems with us. I'm surprised that you, Peter, have not seen the point of our decision as it affects *you*. Mr Last thought you a very promising pupil, and there's no reason why you, too, should not hope to pass the scholarship and go to the big school, infinitely better than anything you could possibly attain to in Hampshire.' I weep hopelessly against my mother's breast, smelling her violet powder. Joan starts crying too, and Bill, not to be outdone, starts a snivelly cry on his own.

'I really do not think,' says my father, 'that I should have to endure all this, when I am doing my level best for you all. Florence, bring youself to an anchor. Peter, you started this, and you should be exceedingly ashamed. I have better news for you, if you will only stop grizzling.'

Florence returns to her chair and rolls another cigarette, the licking of the gummed edge a bit less accurate than usual. I don't seem to be able to stop crying, but I try, and the sobs become slowly more distant and hiccupy.

'I have found new furnished lodgings with ample room for all of us at Shepherds Bush, number 239A Goldhawk Road, and we shall stay there for a few months until my business prospects improve, and we can look for better quarters. Come on, Peter,' he says cajolingly, 'Cheer up! Rome was not built in a day.'

'I will not have your mother made unhappy. We shall be

moving on Saturday next and you three children will have good London schools to attend, which will prepare you for your scholarships far better than the little school at Owslebury. You *must* learn that the path of life is not *all* roses. We shall all be sad to leave the cottage – I include your Mother and myself – but *ultimately*' (beautiful and mysterious word, I think) 'ultimately we shall all benefit from the change.'

In the hollow of my heart, which has been asking desperately *never, never* again? (Cobb's Corner and Jackman's Hill and the Field of the Runcible Cow and Sally Hunney and the Last boys and Bobby Botwright and never again Havertons' farm and my Skippers and Hawkmoths and yellowhammers and swallows and Frankie Southgate and the three thorn trees.) I begin, punctured with small distancing sobs, to wonder whether Shepherd's Bush might be almost in the country, and Goldhawk Road sounds full of trees – how else could it have got its name? And the school, my father says, that we shall go to next Monday is called Brackenbury Road Elementary School: more promises of country life. Lever Street is exciting and strange, but only because we were going back to the cottage and the plum tree and the Medder. A small faint last sob as I think of my walk – now seen to be the last, the last – along Gough's Lane, and there weren't even any Comma butterflies and the Painted Lady was a male, and now never – never again.

'You, Peter, will be able to go every weekend to the Natural History Museum,' continues my father, 'if, of course, you should wish to. You should not treat such prospects with contumely. I shall be able to see you every evening and watch your progress in your studies and – we'll read books aloud, and be cosy together, and you'll soon forget about Owslebury, because life will be so interesting and exciting in London. Theatres, Maskelyne and Devant's, the Crystal Palace, cinemas, libraries – a better life for us all.' He lights a fag gravely. 'There is no need to repine' (a new word: I tried it soundlessly on my tongue – 'repine'). 'If you will trust me to look after your best interests, and, indeed, those of Your Mother, all will be well, and you will not regret the change – which, I remind you again, was decided on entirely and exclusively on your behalf.'

A faint doubt creeps into my mind: is the real reason that they are hard up, and all this stuff about Joan's education pretence? He puts his dying home-made fag into the little brass ashtray, gets up, and plants a wet kiss on each of our foreheads. 'And now I hear Mrs Mullins calling us for supper. My dear Florence, would you care to precede me downstairs?'

So down we go, Florence, Arthur, Joan and me and a reasonably cheerful Bill. And through the stew and pancakes which rather splendidly follow, the incredulity settles into my stomach. I watch my father and Mr Mullins toasting each other in the already familiar beer, Mrs Mullins fussing and leaning and offering more food, and Joan, still faintly proud, accepting another pancake; the thought echoes still through my mind – never, never again. I eat a lot, half-consciously making up for loss elsewhere.

Soon we are taken up to bed, after kisses all round, the Mullinses, my father, everyone except Charleen, the day being regarded as an exhausting one. Joan helps Bill to undress while Florence, bless her, helps me. 'Are you sure the postman will look after my butterflies?' I ask her as she pulls on my pyjama trousers, a faint sob still in my voice. 'They break easily.'

'Don't worry, Pete,' says Florence. 'It'll be all right, I promise you – and if they don't you'll be able to collect some more. It's only a short journey on the Met. to open country and there'll be butterflies in the parks and perhaps in our own garden when we have a proper one. I know how you feel, but in a few days everything will be different, and West London is much more open than this. Goodnight now, and sleep well, both of you. Joan won't be long – she's gone down to talk to Daddy about her new school. Night night – sweet repose.'

I lie in my overstuffed bed trying hard to get my mind off Owslebury, but it tends to come back, like an image at the far end of a telescope held the wrong way round – tiny, sharp, bright, remote, for ever lost. The word 'never' makes a little heartbeat of its own, and I remember last term having to learn my first Scottish song *The Banks of Doon.* The Owslebury version of the Scots accent notwithstanding, the poem suddenly has a new meaning, intensified by the sound.

Thou minds me o' deparrted joys
Depar-arted neverr to-o rreturrn.

I fall asleep hoping that Shepherds Bush (lovely name!) will be beautiful and Goldhawk Road full of trees and flowers and open skies.

Goldhawk Road and Shepherds Bush, I'm afraid, didn't live up to their names, and I never did get my collections from Owslebury. It was not until twenty-eight years later that I left London to live once more in rural surroundings. My father, whatever his immediate motives, was entirely right about my education: I did get to a good school, and subsequently to university. But there was a residual need throughout that period to go back to the country – a need fixed in me for ever by the Hampshire years. I don't think I could ever again live happily in a big town. My bit of Suffolk is beautiful enough for me to feel only faint tremors of nostalgia for downs and beech hangers and the flora of the chalk.

The break with Owslebury was one of the most important events of my life. Perhaps after all we must inevitably 'weep for what is gone'.